Memphis Press-Scimitar

U. S. WEATHER FORECAST: Fair, not quite so cool this afternoon, tonight. Partly cloudy, warmer Saturday. Sunday: Considerable cloudiness, warmer.

FINAL EDITION MARKETS
PRICE FIVE CENTS

68TH YEAR   MEMPHIS, TENN., FRIDAY, AUGUST 6, 1948   NO. 244

Complete Shelby Returns Add To Browning, Kefauver Leads

23 City and 4 County Boxes to Kefauver, Six to Browning

Both Cut Deeply In Total Vote: McCord, Mitchell Carry Shelby

Candidates supported by E. H. Crump for the governorship and Senate nomination received winning totals in Shelby County but these were insufficient to overcome the statewide vote.

The heavy Shelby Coun ;y vote for Estes Kefauver was a major factor in Kefauver's victory.

Kefauver carried 23 city precincts and four county boxes and tied one.

Browning carried three city boxes and three county boxes.

Browning's 20,365 was twice as big a total as any Crump-opposed candidate had received before, as far back as figures were available today.

Complete returns in the gubernatorial race from Shelby's 128 precincts give:

BROWNING	20,365
M'CORD	48,189

From the same precincts, results for the senatorial nomination:

KEFAUVER	77,589
MITCHELL	37,771
STEWART	2,133

What Kefauver, Browning Did in Shelby

Gov. McCord polled 36,893 votes in the city and 11,296 in the county.

Browning's city vote was 16,682. In the county he got 3683.

Kefauver got 72,950 in the city and 4619 in the county. Mitchell received 28,060 in the city and 9711 in the county.

Sen. Stewart polled 2146 in the city and 568 in the county.

GORDON BROWNING

ESTES KEFAUVER

McCord Was Never Ahead: Senate Race Closer

A Double Defeat for E. H. Crump, His First Loss in 20 Years

By CLARK PORTEOUS, Press-Scimitar Staff Writer

The Democratic electorate of Tennessee today had dealt E. H. Crump and his Memphis machine a double defeat by nominating Gordon Browning for governor and Estes Kefauver for U. S. Senator.

That marked the first time in 20 years that the Shelby County political organization has lost a gubernatorial election, and the first time in 22 years that Crump's organization has lost a voting precinct in Memphis in a race in which Crump had definitely indorsed candidates. (In 1936, Cordell Hull carried Shelby despite what he called in his Memoirs "the enmity of the political bosses"—Crump and Luke Lea. However, no formal indorsement was made by the Shelby organization in that race; the Hull understood that Crump was against him.)

The Shelby machine lost one rural box in 1938, when Browning was defeated for re-election by Prentice Cooper. But not since 1926 had the Crump organization lost a city box in a state-wide election. Yesterday it lost 26 in the city, three in the county and there was one tie.

Judge Mitchell Third in Race

Both the Crump-backed candidates—Gov. Jim Nance McCord who was seeking a third term and Judge John A. Mitchell who sought the U. S. Senate nomination—were trailing far behind today on the basis of nearly complete unofficial returns. Senator Tom Stewart, who was jettisoned by Crump, was running far ahead of Mitchell, the machine candidate.

In the governor's race, the returns from 2010 of Tennessee's 2250 voting places showed:

BROWNING	$15,000
M'CORD	176,123

In the Senate primary, with 2010 precincts reporting:

KEFAUVER	158,877
STEWART	115,369
MITCHELL	85,860

Of the 21 counties in West Tennessee area, west of the Tennessee River, in which The Press-Scimitar circulates, Browning carried 16 and Kefauver 13. The races were close in several other counties. Stewart carried eight of these 21 counties and Mitchell carried two—Dyer and Shelby.

The Democratic nomination usually is tantamount to election. Both Browning and Kefauver are due to have Republican opposition in the general election Nov. 2.

In the Republican primary also held yesterday, B. Carroll Reece, former congressman and until recently chairman of the Republican National Committee, easily won the GOP nomination for governor. Hilly Roscoe Roy Acuff won the GOP gubernatorial nomination as easily as he does for fiddle. Win losses of a Republican presidential victory, the Republicans probably will campaign actively for the two state-wide offices.

See-Saw Battle for the Senate

Gordon Browning was tired and sound men making talks on behalf of a little houses after more than of their candidates. Some of the 160 stump speeches—but he was citizens went to alter parts of the calm and made talks. state and made talks.

"It was a wonderful victory," The two candidates backed Judge he told The Press-Scimitar via Nashville headquarters.

"The people was a kid" and anxious as I can be to justify their action—"I'm going to too right care."

"I am not immediate plan?" he said.

"Fraser delayed comment early today when asked if he was still under in action—"Well, I'm ready to go yet, I'll make a statement later," he said.

McCord was never ahead at any time from the first precinct to the last, but the vote between Kefauver and Stewart see-sawed back and forth all night. As returns piled up it appeared Kefauver was building to lead total. At mid-evening, his margin was several thousand votes. Other Congressmen from Tennessee conceded.

Coal Mine Tragedy

WELCH, W. Va., Aug. 6 — Five men were killed and nine injured today in a slate fall at in the New River and Pocahontas Consolidated Coal Co. at Capels, near here.

Where to Find It—

Turn to Page 3—BROWNING

Losing Candidates Concede Defeat

By United Press

NASHVILLE, Aug. 6 — Sen. Tom Stewart and Gov. Jim McCord conceded defeat in their respective races today.

Stewart offered congratulations to Winner Estes Kefauver and added: "I am sorry to have lost the race but I am extremely grateful to my friends and supporters throughout the state.

McCord pledged his support to Winner Gordon Browning, saying:

"I entered the contest for a third term because of my interest in the welfare of the state and suggested under my administration, and I propose to take the same tax for four years as I have in the past two years and I am proud of my record as governor of Tennessee."

All of Kefauver's friends were jubilant today. Browning sent his congratulations to Kefauver.

Kefauver's break—

"Open the hands of stimulating Memphis a victory today."

"I entered the contest for a third term because of my interest in the welfare of the state and suggested under my Democratic nomination for the U. S. Senate.

Judge John Mitchell issued this Shelby statement today:

"Upon the basis of unofficial figures I realize I have been defeated in my race for the United States Senate, and I congratulate my opponent, Estes Kefauver. There is nothing to feel badly about for the people of the state have spoken and their decision must be respected."

Turn to Page 3—KEFAUVER

'Private Housing' Gets the Nod

Senate Rejects Truman Idea

By United Press

WASHINGTON Aug 4. The senate, with the July. subsidizing firmly in the public relief since housing bill designed to encourage private home building...

By its action, the senate rejected President Truman's plea for a housing program that would include public construction and slum clearance.

The house has passed a housing bill quite similar to the final senate version. Differences will be ironed out in conference.

The Senate Banking Committee tore down a last-ditch effort in Mr. Truman wage and price controls. It approved instead an anti-inflation bill limited to mild controls on bank and consumer credit. The house has passed a similar bill.

Acting Republic Leader Kenneth S. Wherry of Nebraska said he is hopeful that Congress can go home tomorrow.

Dogs Go After Lost Children

Pet Finds One Finds the Other

ZANESVILLE, Ohio, Aug 6 — Three-year-old Jerry Lee Huffman, missing all night, was found at 7 a.m. today trapped in a mire farm where his Collie dog led searchers to the area.

The child was named and almost unconscious from exposure. His feet was caught in the mire after a wild grape-vine had twisted about his body. He had left his clothes in his yard, about two miles away.

MILTON, Mass Aug 6 — Four-year-old Francis Reidy who wandered away from a berry picking party yesterday in the Blue Hills reservation, was found alive today after an 18-hour search. The boy was tracked down by the reservation police dog Rover.

House Bloodhounds Off On a Hot Spy-Hunt

Mystery Witness Being Questioned in Secret—Senate Closes Hearing

By CHARLES T. LUCEY, Scripps-Howard Staff Writer

WASHINGTON, Aug. 6 — It is a sure thing the committee said he has work was into Elizabeth T. Bentl husted up a witness who might fire the Vassar girl who took a break the whole Russian espionage lift up in Communists probed the story wide open at next week. A mysterious witness being questioned in a committee is now interviewing the biggest spy yarn in years.

Today Rep. Karl Mundt (Rep., S. D.), acting chairman of the House Un-American Activities Committee, pulled a firing pin of his own.

The subcommittee was supposed to leave last night, arrive at its destination by noon today start questioning the mystery man this afternoon and get back to Washington tomorrow.

Senators who are investigating Communist spy ring charges today suspended their public hearings because they said the Truman administration refuses to give them necessary facts.

Chairman Ferguson (Rep., Mich.) of the Senate Investigating Subcommittee charged the Truman administration is making political capital out of the investigation.

Here is a summary of the fantastic, many-sided story as it has unraveled in seven days:

On a previous day's Miss Bentley—Louis Budenz, the ex-editor of the Daily Worker and Whittaker Chambers, a senior editor of Time Magazine—all severally from Communist-confessed that her years ago entrained the U S Government service.

These spies, it was testified were able to get important political and military information from government files, touching on our production and aircraft formulas, and funnel it into Moscow.

They were aided, according to testimony made before the House Un-American Committee Thursday and. Ferguson s committee, by government officials of the Roosevelt Administration who were named.

Turn to Page 3—SPY HUNT

3 Congressmen Claim Victory

Phillips, Jennings And Courtney

By United Press

NASHVILLE Tenn. Aug 6 — Three Tennessee congressmen two Republicans and a Democrat apparently won renomination in six districts races primaries.

Rep. Dayton E. Phillips held a vote of 27,614 to 9424 for William K. Miller Johnson City lawyer on unofficial returns from 267 of the 331 precincts in the First Congressional District (Republican) were tabulated.

Rep. John Jennings with lead in the Republican race in the Second District in unofficial returns that 178 Knoxville lawyer who opposed him in the Republican primary.

In the Third District James E. Frazier former U. S. District attorney of Chattanooga won the nomination in Democrat in representing the district now served by Rep. Estes Kefauver.

Frazier defeated Wade Dutton Commission from Chattanooga nominees and votes leader The district's 361 precincts gave Frazier 11,706, Hammer 18,986 and Moore 440.

Other Congressmen from Tennessee apparently renominated.

New Record Vote for Shelby County

A new record for a Shelby County primary was total was set. In the governorship race the vote was 66,412.

In the senate race the vote was 99,459.

The record vote in 1926 was 85,874, when Frank Lowndes Hall defeated Browning for re-election as governor.

The 1940 precincts was known as Gummer's Horse's had a pretty close race Shelby, Gov. McCord and for Senator Al McKellar.

With a few exceptions such as Stewartville and Morning Sun, where the voting was overwhelmingly one-sided for the machine, the voting blurred the city's rural precincts. However, one rural box—Crump-backed Mitchell's right over Kefauver was true-blue 5 to 4.

Three stroke-by votes were recorded. In Ward 36 Precinct 7 the town of E.T; Trafford was willing to as the 32 per cent that all the voters around...

Both in the gubernatorial race there were Crump-backed Mitchell's right over Kefauver 40 to 5.

Stewart a strongest showing in Shelby was in Ward 34, Precinct 9...

FCC Asks $64 Query: Radio Quiz Programs Must Reply

Wants to Know If Guessing Shows Don't Violate Airlane Lottery Laws

By United Press

WASHINGTON Aug 6 — The Federal Communications Commission today put the nation's quiz programs and the big lottery and quiz programs on notice to answer a vital question by ten days or else it will assume to answer to be an act violation.

The question was: Why shouldn't the Commission, two most of these programs be prohibited at the Radio Lottery Law?

The Commission yesterday issued a rule "is the effect, the FCC charge was so broad that it would apply to ordinary programs do not violate the Federal Communications Act Fe; 316.

The major networks explained today role will go into effect unless some one can convince the Padtem--dest...

In several all interrupted parties networks sponsors before dismission in the statements at which will in being broadcast by the Commission by Sept. 25.

The Commission headed three the broadcasters ruling it a step in waiving Blanket W A N L Arlington ... Va. It held that most station's telephones were received to not...

Morning Chilly, Warm to Come

Yellow Cab Signs New Drivers' Pact

The Yellow Cab Co. signed a new contract the last steps with its Memphis Yellow Cab Drivers' Association, concluding a month of friendly negotiations F. E. Galton ...

The main provisions in the new agreement involve radio cab drivers will receive 40 per cent of the meter take after an 18-hour search.

Drivers carried across lines at bride pick. Bloodhounds had been put on the trail but Frank Lebrun a breaker, first spotted the youngster.

Can You Answer?

(Answers on Page 3)

1. President Truman recently designated February 1 as National Freedom Day. Why?

2. THE STAR is the name under which former New York tabloid that was recently sold by Marshall Field?

3. Seven letters in the alphabet are used in the Roman numerals, how many can you name?

4. What date in January 1948 commences the next term of office for the U. S. President?

5. Name the first woman to retire the English Channel, who performs this feat twice?

Gold Sea Kills Tots

BERLIN, Aug. 6 — Seven German children, from two to 14 years old perished at Cloppie while playing yesterday in the Baltic near Heilig, and eight others rescued German game until late sea.

The River Stage

The Mississippi River 13.0 feet at Memphis today, a fall of 0.2 foot.

Amazing Estes Broke Rules But Wound Up Winning With Help of Memphis

By RICHARD WALLACE, Press-Scimitar Staff Writer

Rep. Estes Kefauver—the Democratic nominee for senator from Tennessee—was the man after one of the most amazing and unorthodox campaigns in the history of Tennessee politics.

Mr. Kefauver broke all the rules by which all the presidential candidates of the Shelby organization. This was written to the public rule—thrown with an old-time political chart.

In the first place, he announced for the senate on the strength of a pledge that he would try to roll up such a majority in the remainder of the state that it would overwhelmed it in

Not so McKeever. He flat made no blanket with his campaign who more severed offenses in June to enter the race—he declared war on Crump. The patient work

Turn to Page 3—KEFAUVER

Broke Shelby Rule

He quickly broke a second "be written" rule among candidates who do not mention any other county—the Shelby organization. This was written rule—throwing—throwing common sense names today shows the Crump machine and all the old crusades today.

Big Three Meets With Molotov

By Associated Press

MOSCOW, Aug. 6 — Envoys of the United States Britain and France had their second lengthy session with Soviet Foreign Minister V. M. Molotov today at which time they and Molotov probed more deeply into the problems of the Berlin and the German question.

When the spokesmen said that were meeting at this session of the diplomats at this conference, the was doing in business for about the foreign ministers.

070.4092
M47e

102536

DATE DUE			

The Editorial We

A Posthumous Autobiography

by

Edward J. Meeman

Compiled, Edited, and with an Introduction and
Afterword by Edwin Howard

Memphis State University Printing Services

For J. Z. H.,
The editor's editor,
with love and gratitude.

Copyright © 1976 by The Edward J. Meeman Foundation
Printed in the United States of America

Library of Congress Cataloging in Publication Data

Meeman, Edward John, 1889–1966.
The editorial we.

1. Meeman, Edward John, 1889–1966. I. Howard,
Edwin, 1924–   II. Title.
PN4874.M485A33   070.4′092′4 [B]   75–40139

Foreword

Edward John Meeman, 1889–1966, spent 59 years of his life in newspaper work—14 years in Indiana and 45 in Tennessee, ending his service as Scripps-Howard Conservation Editor for four years. Born to a poor family, he did not inherit money. He did not marry money—he was never married at all, except to his profession.

To him, his profession was more than just publishing the news and commenting on it—it was public service; not merely doing something for the public, but stimulating the people to do things for themselves.

Personally, he was generous but thrifty. He saved much of his salary, and made successful investments, so that on his death he left a fortune of more than $2,000,000.

In 1949, he created the Edward J. Meeman Foundation, bequeathing to it the major part of his estate, charging it with the task of spending his money in the interest of better journalism, of conservation of natural resources, and of greater participation by the people in public affairs. The Meeman Foundation, having disbursed most of Meeman's fortune in this manner, presents this book as a picture of the man, his career and his ideas and beliefs.

On November 3, 1973, Meeman was inducted by the Tennessee Press Association into the Tennessee Newspaper

Hall of Fame. Selections for this honor are made by TPA past presidents from among prominent journalists who have been dead five years or more. In its citation of Meeman, the Tennessee Press Association said:

Edward J. Meeman was a gentle but forceful champion of causes.

His good works have lived on after his death through the Edward J. Meeman Foundation . . . The Foundation has given conservation prizes annually, has made major grants to the University of Tennessee, Memphis State University and other institutions to encourage journalism education, and continues to present awards (originally established by Meeman himself) to Tennessee newsmen and women for excellence in editorials and public service.

While editor of *The Knoxville News-Sentinel,* Meeman fought a corrupt city government . . . and brought about a change to a council-manager government. He campaigned for flood control, agricultural improvement and development of public power along the Tennessee River, laying the foundation for the establishment of the Tennessee Valley Authority. Meeman was a prime mover in the conservation of natural resources efforts that culminated in the creation of the Great Smoky Mountains National Park.

He became editor of *The Memphis Press-Scimitar* in 1931, took on the Memphis political boss, E. H. Crump, and after 17 years of battling saw the end of boss rule with the passage of laws repealing the poll tax and setting up permanent voter registration and the use of voting machines.

He led in advocating civil rights, better agricultural and conservation practices, and worked through his paper and privately to encourage the government to purchase 12,500 acres of land in Shelby County for a state park. After his death, this forest was named Meeman-Shelby Forest State Park in his honor.

Contents

Introduction

What makes an editor important?

The editors of the *New York Times*, the *New York Daily News*, the *Chicago Tribune*, the *Washington Post*, the *Los Angeles Times*, the *Philadelphia Bulletin*, the *Detroit News*, and a few other such gargantuan journalistic enterprises, are important because of their newspapers' strategic locations and large circulations. Because these editors speak to and, presumably, for, large numbers of people in key population, business, industrial, and governmental centers, whatever they say in their editorial columns gains weight from the mastheads over them. Whoever they are, whatever they represent, such editors are heard. Their newspapers make them important.

In the almost 300-year history of American journalism, there have been a few editors who were important not because of the newspapers they headed, but because of what they had to say. The late William Allen White of the *Emporia* (Kansas) *Gazette* was widely recognized as that kind of editor. So was Hodding Carter of the Greenville, Mississippi, *Delta Democrat-Times*. Not so widely recognized during his lifetime was Edward J. Meeman, editor of *The Memphis Press-Scimitar*, a Scripps-Howard newspaper. Like White's and Carter's, Meeman's voice—as I will demonstrate—was heard and heeded in the halls of power and decision. Like them, he lent weight to his paper's masthead. Like them, he made his newspaper important.

Will White first gained a nationwide audience in 1896 at the age of 28 with a slashing attack on William Jennings Bryan, the Democratic Party (whose presidential nominee Bryan was), and the Populists. His biting editorial, "What's the Matter With Kansas?" was picked up by Chicago papers and widely distributed by the Republican Party. In the remaining half-century that he edited the *Emporia Gazette*, with its 7000 daily circulation, his colorful, direct, and often acerbic editorials were read by congressmen and presidents.

But despite his prominence and influence, White remained a commentator rather than a leader. In his 1947 biography, *William Allen White's America*, Walter Johnson wrote: "The Emporia editor was not an original or creative thinker. He was no great iconoclast, or revolutionary, no risky radical. Had he been such, he would not have become a folk hero." But a hero he was, often mentioned in the same breath with Will Rogers. His prop was a pen instead of a lariat, and his platform a printing press rather than the stage, but the folksy sentiments and common sense were much the same. As the *Washington Post* put it after his death: " . . . generally speaking, he was the national thermometer rather than the penicillin."

The late Hodding Carter didn't have the folksy touch, but he did have White's flair for personal journalism and for attracting national attention to himself and his 12,000-circulation newspaper. Returning from the editorship of the Middle East editions of the Army's *Stars & Stripes* newspaper and *Yank* magazine, Carter won the Pulitzer Prize in 1946 for his series of editorials on racial, religious and economic tolerance. His editorials and magazine articles made him one of the chief spokesmen for the liberal Southern view during the early days of the Civil Rights debate. In his newspaper, he battled Mississippi Senator Theodore Bilbo and the state legislature, which venomously attacked him for his moderate racial position. Simply being on the other side of the racial fence from his attackers was enough to make Carter a favorite of Eastern Liberal magazine editors.

Like White, Carter mirrored more than he shaped the enlightened middle-class opinion of his area and era. Both gained national audiences as editors, but won national note primarily as writers, through their books and magazine articles.

Without the folksiness of White or the magazine outlets of Carter, Edward J. Meeman for 31 years made *The Memphis Press-Scimitar* one of the most influential newspapers in middle America, that vast and varied land which lies between and beyond the great urban centers of population and structured power. For 25 years before that, Meeman was a reporter and managing editor on the *Evansville*, (Indiana), *Press*, reporter for the *Terre Haute* (Indiana) *Times* and the Newspaper Enterprise Association, and founder and editor of the *Knoxville* (Tennessee) *News-Sentinel*. It was during those years that he developed, tested, and dedicated himself to the ethical principles and public service policies which were to make him and *The Press-Scimitar* great forces for local, regional, national and international good during the '30's, '40's, and '50's.

More than any other editor, it was Meeman who put the National Park in the Great Smoky Mountains, put the authority in the Tennessee Valley Authority, and took the Boss out of Boss Crump.

He was a crusading editor who picked his causes not on odds, but on merit. He didn't always win. In 1964 he fought, against his own newspaper concern's policy, to get the United States out of Vietnam. In a personal letter to President Lyndon B. Johnson, in an editorial distributed by Scripps-Howard Newspaper Alliance even though its editors disagreed with it, in personal letters to those editors, and in an article published in the *Freedom & Union* magazine, Meeman urged:

"The only way to avoid (a new isolationism) is not to sink deeper in the Vietnam morass but to get out. When you start to sink in a swamp, the thing to do is get out before you sink over your head. Get out!

"There is no military victory in Asia we might win which will give us a peace we can manage, but the sooner we make peace on the best terms we can get, the sooner we will get out of a situation that becomes more dangerous to our cause the longer we are there.

"It is said our prestige will suffer if we give up in Vietnam. Not as badly as if we pursue an impossible adventure to its bitter, bitter end, when more than our prestige will suffer."

Earlier, Meeman's editorial leadership had put unity into the Atlantic Union by piloting the citizens' movement that put Estes Kefauver in the U.S. Senate. Kefauver's death took some of the wind out of that movement's sails, but the ecological breeze Meeman stirred up as Scripps-Howard Conservation Editor is blowing with ever-increasing force.

It was Meeman's leadership that got the Wilderness Bill and the Land and Water Conservation Fund Bill through Congress in 1964, a fact recognized by the National Wildlife Federation's bestowing its Communications Award on him that year.

Of course, Meeman didn't do any of these things alone, as he was always the first to point out. In every cause, he marshaled the full resources of his staff to get the facts and sought citizen support from key individuals and groups. He was never a mere voice crying in the wilderness. When Scripps-Howard Newspapers presented him the Roy W. Howard Award in 1960 for "exceptional initiative and enterprise," the citation read: "His Faith in the Human Spirit Inspired These Newpapers to Win Many a 'Lost Cause.'"

His guiding principle as a crusading editor was best expressed in a simple maxim he formulated, tested, and repeatedly proved:

"Citizens working alone can do much; a newspaper work-

ing alone can do much; citizens and their newspapers working together can do anything."

He was never an "I" editor. He always spoke with the editorial "We." Included in that first-person plurality were *The Press-Scimitar's* top reporters and editors and the Mid-South's most informed and enlightened citizens, a plurality which grew dynamically through the years of Meeman's editorial leadership.

When he died on November 15, 1966, at the age of 77, in the comfortable bedroom of his beloved Forest Farm just outside Memphis, Meeman was best-known beyond the Mid-South for his accomplishments as a conservationist. On learning of his death, the wife of the President of the United States, Mrs. Lyndon B. Johnson, said:

"The voice and pen of Mr. Meeman have been stilled. But his invaluable work over many years in conservation is a lasting legacy to all Americans. Through his efforts we shall all be richer in the beauty of our land." And Secretary of the Interior Stewart Udall said: ". . . for many years he was the leading voice for conservation in the mid-continent area. Over the years, his crusades for conservation resulted in landmark decisions which have affected the face of the continent and enhanced the future for all citizens."

Decades before the word "ecology" came into vogue, Meeman was advocating and working effectively for the conservation of our natural resources—the preservation of forests, the enrichment of soil, and the purification of air, oceans, rivers, lakes and streams. The Great Smoky Mountains National Park, TVA, Meeman-Shelby Forest State Park, *The Press-Scimitar's* annual S.O.S. (Save-enrich Our Soil) campaigns and prizes, the annual $5000 or more Meeman Conservation Awards given through the Scripps-Howard Foundation, and the passage of innumerable state and federal conservation acts all stand as proof of his advocacy and action in the field of ecology.

TVA and the Great Smokies Park are two of the brightest

stars in Meeman's crown. For more than eight years before the Tennessee Valley Authority was established in 1933, Meeman had fought for flood and erosion control and public power development on the Tennessee River through the construction of a dam on Cove Creek, now the site of the TVA's Norris Dam.

He cited in his paper the success of public power at Seattle and Niagara. By 1930, through his and others' efforts, Congress had been so impressed that both houses passed a bill providing for a government dam at Cove Creek. Meeman had been in Washington for the final push. Leaving, he found President Herbert Hoover on the train with him. Hoover was known to be dubious about the Cove Creek project. Meeman discussed the just-passed bill with him, and got a promise from him that he would not veto the bill. Elated, Meeman got off the train and wired the good news to his paper in Knoxville, which printed the story under a page one banner-line. But—Hoover, nevertheless, pocket-vetoed the bill, so the development of the Tennessee River for power, flood-control and conservation had to wait three years for President Franklin D. Roosevelt and Senator George W. Norris and their leadership which brought about the TVA.

Later, when TVA needed one large city as a power customer to make it a success, Meeman put on a campaign which brought TVA to Memphis. Today, TVA is wholesale power supplier to 162 local electric systems serving two million customers in parts of seven states, and sells power directly to several large atomic, military and industrial installations. By 1970, its power sales amounted to about 60 times as much electricity as the region was using when TVA was founded in 1933. TVA operates 26 major dams of its own on the Tennessee River and its tributaries, and by agreement with the Aluminum Company of America controls water releases at six of its major dams. These structures, besides generating power, control flood waters and make the main stream of the Tennessee navigable over its entire 650-mile length. Byproducts of incalculable value include vast recreational facilities and the development of agricultural, forestry, and water quality resources. Despite several assaults on its autonomy, including one by Tennessee's late Senator K.D McKellar, against which Meeman vigorously fought, TVA's power distribution remains financially self-supporting and its power bonds self-liquidating.

In his book, *Strangers in High Places*, Michael Frome writes; "The Smoky Mountains are the national park that came into being as a testament of man's faith, and not without sacrifice and struggle," and adds of this most-visited park in the nation: "In Knoxville, Edward J. Meeman, editor of *The Knoxville News-Sentinel*, was an instrumental figure in the Smoky Mountain park movement."

Later, after being struck during a visit to Germany by the beauty and accessibility of that country's state parks, Meeman led the movement which gave Memphis a 12,500-acre state park on its northern doorstep—a wonderful wild-life and forest preserve and recreational facility which now bears his name.

But Edward J. Meeman was no one-note editor. He sang with equal fire and fervor the anthem of good government on the local, state, national and international levels. As a young reporter and editor in Indiana, he exposed public graft and a boss-controlled legislature, and fought determinedly, if unsuccessfully, to bring council-manager government to Evansville. As an editor in Knoxville, he fought the council-manager battle over again—and won.

In Memphis, he accomplished what alone should have earned him immortality as an editor but did not even, to the discredit of the selections committee, win him a Pulitzer Prize. Moving to the city in 1931, he found it completely, and willingly, dominated by the political machine headed by the late E.H. Crump. It was the most absolute dictatorship that ever controlled an American city—Jersey City, Kansas City, New York, Chicago, and Boston included.

Born in Holly Springs, Mississippi, 45 miles south of Memphis, in 1874, Crump had left home at 16 to keep books for

a country store in Lula, Mississippi. A year later, the "Red
Snapper" (so named for his red hair and biting comebacks)
moved into the much larger arena of Memphis as clerk in a
cotton office, then bookkeeper for the Woods-Chickasaw
Saddlery Co. Within six years, he had taken over and made it
the E.H. Crump Buggy & Harness Co.

After marrying a young woman of wealth and social position, Crump made his political debut in 1901 as a successful
reform candidate for the city council. Unable to exert much
influence there, he resigned and a week later ran for the Board
of Fire & Police Commissioners, and won. Within weeks, he
had contrived to force all saloons to close by midnight. Winning
the office of mayor by 79 votes, he clamped down on open
gambling, but it continued to flourish underground. Gaming
operators of the time claimed they had to hand over 40 per cent
of their take to continue operating on the QT.

By Meeman's arrival in Memphis in 1931, Crump and his
machine were solidly entrenched and the citizens of Memphis
seemed content to have him run their business as well as his
own thriving insurance company. He had by this time turned
Memphis into one of the cleanest, quietest, and most effi-
ciently operated cities in the country. Crump himself was
colorful and exciting—for most citizens, a prized possession,
like the river. It was a city in which liberty and democracy were
so dead that most people didn't miss it. The Boss seemed
unbeatable.

As Ralph G. Martin wrote in his 1964 book, *The Bosses*,
". . . The corruption of Edward Hull Crump was a clean corruption. The gangrene was there, but it never smelled, seldom
showed—it was in the core.

"As the most benevolent political boss in the business,
Crump gave Memphians good government, but the price was
high. The price was the destruction of the basic essence of
democracy—the right of choice. So complete was the Crump
control for a quarter of a century that the people of Memphis
could either vote for a Crump candidate, or not at all.

"And the democratic tragedy was the lack of democracy, the fact that most Memphians couldn't care less about their vote. . . . That was the root of the rottenness—not the Crump power, but the public indifference. . . . . "

Meeman, as new editor of *The Memphis Press-Scimitar*, immediately took his stand against the machine and the boss who ran it. But like the great editorial general he was, he picked his battlegrounds judiciously, mapped them meticulously, and used his fire-power selectively.

More than Crump himself, Meeman attacked the public indifference which made his power possible. His strategy was to convince the people of Memphis that they were free—free to govern themselves, free to choose democracy over a paternalistic but oppressive dictatorship, free to create a better government than the machine, for all its pretensions of efficiency, could provide—and to make them want to exercise that freedom.

It took him 17 years to do it. During those years, marked by bitter personal attacks on Meeman, the worst always voiced by Crump puppets while the Boss pulled their strings, Meeman often said that if any 10 men who were well regarded by their fellow citizens would band together to resist and oppose the machine, it would be defeated. When the time came, in 1948, it took only seven, by Meeman's count, though with characteristic modesty he failed to count himself.

The downfall of the Crump machine came about as the result of Estes Kefauver's victorious campaign for the U.S. Senate. When the 6-foot-3, 215-pound congressman from Madisonville, Tennessee, had the audacity to seek the Senate seat without Crump's support, the Boss took out full-page newspaper ads contemptuously labeling him a "pet coon" who would "steal while looking the other way." With a grin, Kefauver simply donned a coonskin cap and, declaring "I'm not Boss Crump's pet coon," headed west seeking support in Crump's own crucial Shelby County. Meeman admired his congressional record, as well as his courage, and worked both behind the scenes and through *The Press-Scimitar's* editorial columns to assemble in Memphis a seven-member Kefauver Committee. During the campaign, the seven maintained they were working "for Kefauver, not against Crump," but Kefauver's election smashed the machine's drive-shaft, and signaled the end of the Crump era—not only locally, but throughout the state. The Crump "colonies," which had sprung up at Athens and other Tennessee places, faded away after 1948, and statewide candidates quit trying to hook on to the Memphis machine.

Kefauver had made a splendid record as Tennessee's Commissioner of Finances and Taxation in 1938 and '39. His revenue reforms were credited with paying off $50-million in state debts and creating a $27-million surplus. As a congressman, he specialized in public power, small business, and congressional reform legislation, and was named one of the 10 best representatives in Congress by *Collier's* magazine.

In the Senate, Kefauver became most famous as chairman of the Senate Crime Investigating Committee in 1950–51. With the same easy courage with which he had faced down Ed Crump, the soft-spoken Tennessean put the finger on such criminal characters as Greasy Thumb Guzik, "The Enforcer," "Dandy Phil," "Jimmy Blue Eyes" and "Trigger Mike." When the political lumberjacks looked over the presidential timber in 1952, there was Estes Kefauver, standing straight and tall. He entered 16 Democratic primaries and won 14 of them. If the delegates to the Democratic Convention had cast their ballots as directed by the primary voters, he would have been unbeatable at the convention. He did lead by 67 votes on the first ballot. But because his nationally televised crime investigation had stepped on some tender toes in the Democratic hierarchy, and because he had announced for the nomination without a by-your-leave from then President Harry S Truman, the tree-tall Tennessee senator was chopped down.

As a senator, however, he was doing what his Memphis supporters had helped elect him to do. Meeman and the

Kefauver Committee had been largely motivated to work for him by his support of Clarence Streit's proposal to form a federal union, like the United States, of the democratic nations on both sides of the Atlantic. With the election of Kefauver and the loosening of the Crump vise on Memphis, Meeman threw his energy and his newspaper's support behind the movement. Within a year, the Memphis chapter of Federal Union, Inc., had more members in proportion to population than any chapter in the country.

On January 9, 1949, before Senator Kefauver had even been sworn in, he and two of his leading Memphis supporters, Lucius E. Burch, Jr. and Edmund Orgill, went with Clarence Streit to call on former Supreme Court Justice Owen J. Roberts, who had been a longtime advocate of a federal union of the free. At that conference, Justice Roberts agreed to lead in the formation of the Atlantic Union Committee, a political action group with headquarters in New York, to back a resolution in Congress for a constitutional convention of the Atlantic democracies. It was the Memphis movement, led by the men Meeman persuaded to support Kefauver, which woke up the then dormant Federal Union idea and translated it into the political sphere.

The Atlantic Union Resolution, with Kefauver's leadership, passed in the Congress and, in 1959, the first Atlantic Congress was held in London. In the American delegation were Edmumd Orgill and Edward J. Meeman of Memphis. Although the Atlantic Union movement suffered a severe setback with the deaths of Senator Kefauver in 1963 and Meeman in 1966, Federal Union, Inc., still functions on an educational, nonpolitical basis, and every now and then a move is made in Congress for another convention of representatives of the NATO countries.

Many who had supported the Crump machine in its heyday, and some of the few who had not, feared that a worse corruption would rush in to fill the vacuum created by the machine's dissolution. But Memphis today is not only freer, but better run, than it was in the Crump years, thanks largely to Meeman and the citizens he attracted to the cause of good government; whereas there were few contestants against the Crump candidates, now there are always many candidates and tickets, and the number of voters in every election is now a far greater percentage of those of voting age than in the old days.

Under the editor's leadership, the Civic Research Committee Inc., a non-political research and educational organization, was formed in 1949 to promote better local government. It was largely responsible for getting home rule for Memphis and Shelby County, permanent voter registration, voting machines and better voting places. It also led the way to County Court reapportionment, the change from commission to mayor-council government, run-off elections for city government, and consolidation of several overlapping city and county agencies, including the tax assessment machinery and the Juvenile Courts. Its other recommendations included: modernization of city planning, and a limited state constitutional convention system, by which the state Constitution—untouched since 1870—was first amended in 1953 and can be amended through successive conventions held not oftener than every six years.

Meeman also led in the establishment in 1959 of the Citizens Association of Memphis and Shelby County, a political action group formed to help implement improvements recommended by the Civic Research Committee. It continued to function, with numerous successes and some failures, until his death.

Meeman was also a key organizer and member of the Memphis Committee on Human Relations, which urged and helped plan and carry out the desegregation of all public facilities in Memphis well in advance of most Southern cities. A quarter-century after Crump's power waned—and nearly a decade after Meeman's death—Memphis thrives under the citizen government the editor was instrumental in establishing.

Like most lifelong journalists, Meeman wrote, in the

course of his 59 year career, the equivalent of many books. (I myself, in a mere 33 years as a reporter and columnist, have had published, at an average of 700 words per working day— 168,000 words a year—a conservatively estimated total of more than 5,000,000 words, or the equivalent of 50 long, or 100 short, novels.) From time to time during his career, Meeman also wrote material intended for publication in book form. A book he titled "Man's Progress" was rejected by several publishers in the '40's. After his "retirement" in 1962, during his four busy years as editor emeritus of *The Press-Scimitar* and conservation editor of Scripps-Howard Newspapers, he revised and added to this material with the idea of publishing two books. At his death, however, both were uncompleted.

Yet this man had written, as I said, the equivalent of many books, and it seemed to me that any reasonably competent editor could find in that wealth of material and arrange into publishable form The Book which Meeman himself might have wished to publish, had he not been too busy, and too modest, to do so. In undertaking to do the job for him, I was motivated by my personal admiration and affection for him, guided by whatever professional judgment and skills were inculcated in me by him, and inspired by a signed editorial column which he wrote for *The Press-Scimitar* on February 17, 1960, and which was subsequently reprinted in many other publications.

Meeman himself felt that his column, headed "The Greatest Editor Who Ever Lived," was one of perhaps half a dozen of his writings which were truly inspired—articles, that is, in which the ideas expressed and the facility and flow of their expression seemed to come from some source outside himself.

(From The Memphis Press-Scimitar, February 17, 1960)

If I were a carpenter, I would be proud that Jesus worked at my trade.

If I were a physician, I would note how important Jesus held the healing of the sick, and glory in my profession.

If I were a psychologist, I would study the words of this

great psychologist, who "knew what was in man"—He knew the evil to be banished, the good to be brought out.

If I were a student, I would note how Jesus, at the age of 12, sought out the teachers and did not wait for the teacher to seek him.

If I were a teacher, I would note how Jesus, himself of little formal education, took ignorant and unlearned men and made them the carriers of the world's highest knowledge, the knowledge of the nature of God, and how to avail oneself of His goodness by obeying His laws.

If I were a lawyer, I would marvel at the most magnificent extemporaneous defense in history; Jesus saying to those who would have trapped him into disloyalty to the Romans, "Render unto Caesar the things that are Caesar's and unto God the things that are God's." And to those who would have trapped him into disloyalty to tradition, he said: "He that is without sin among you, let him cast the first stone."

If I were a minister, I would study the Sermon on the Mount and emulate it. And I would remember that it is not recorded that Jesus had a manuscript or even used notes.

If I were an organizer, I would see in Jesus the greatest of organizers, who took 12 ordinary men, and with these inadequate instruments, established the beginning of the Kingdom of Heaven on earth, which continues to this day.

But I am an editor, and I see Jesus as incomparably the greatest editor who ever lived.

He found, in two separate places in the Old Testament, two statements:

In Deuteronomy he found: "Thou shalt love the Lord thy God with all thy heart, and with all thy soul, and with all thy might."

Turning back to Leviticus, he found the words: "Thou shalt love thy neighbor as thyself."

He put them together.

He added the word "mind" before putting them together. What a stroke of divinely inspired genius! For our goodness is of no avail unless we use our reason. As the scholar, the late John Erskine, said, we have "a moral duty to be intelligent." And as the man on the street says, we should "use the sense God gave us."

And so the words emerged in a form so perfect that nothing

need be added to them to make a statement of all there is, or can be, to religion:—(The rest is but elaboration or exposition):

"Thou shalt love the Lord thy God with all thy heart, and with all thy soul, and with all thy mind.

"This is the first and great commandment.

"And the second is like unto it. Thou shalt love thy neighbor as thyself.

"On these two commandments hang all the law and the prophets".

A great editor finds what is most significant. He adds what is necessary for completeness. He arranges the words in the order that they can best be understood and valued.

And so Jesus stands as the greatest editor who ever lived, the pattern and example for all editors everywhere who may humbly seek to follow in his footsteps.

". . . A great editor finds what is most significant. He adds what is necessary for completeness. He arranges the words in the order that they can be best understood and valued . . ."

In this posthumous autobiography of one of the greatest editors of our time, those are the things I have tried to do. This is, in every sense, his book—the book of his life, which was uniquely and solely devoted to his work, which was, in turn, completely dedicated to the welfare of others.

I lived with Edward J. Meeman, as he was reflected in his writings, for more than a year and a half. I began with 17 cardboard boxes filled with file-folders of unpublished manuscripts, clippings, tear sheets, speeches and letters, which I reduced to 33 folders and manila envelopes of material, only a fraction of which—one fat file-folder—could be used in the final manuscript. I hope and believe this book of his life contains the essence of Edward J. Meeman as he was able to express his being through the written word. Although I knew him as friend and employer for more than 20 years and had been awed by his forceful presence when I was a small child and my father, Zollie Howard, was his star reporter and city editor in Knoxville, I found that I did not really know the dedicated, generous, courageous, questioning, searching, confident, self-doubting, incisive, naive, friendly, withdrawn—in short, immensely complicated—man reflected in all those articles, editorials, speeches, memos, letters, poems and personal reminiscences.

He started his professional life as a $4-a-week reporter and ended it as the dean of Scripps-Howard editors and a leading Scripps-Howard stockholder who had accumulated an estate valued at over $2-million. He started his political life as a Socialist who profoundly admired Eugene V. Debs and who would say, in introducing the five-time presidential candidate at a party meeting in Evansville, Indiana, in 1911: "We are proud of this great prophet of industrial righteousness. And how we love him. We love him for making us his friends, but we also love him for the enemies he has made . . ." He ended as a political independent who supported the capitalist system but believed fervently that it needed reforming; for years, he had tried unsuccessfully to persuade Scripps-Howard to institute profit-sharing.

Socialist Debs, whom Meeman knew personally, was one of the stronger influences on his life. Born in Terre Haute, Indiana, Debs, as a young locomotive fireman, organized the American Railway Union and led it in a historic strike against the Pullman Company in Chicago in 1894. A contempt of court citation sent him to Woodstock (Ill.) prison for six months, made a hero of him, and enough of a national figure to run for President in 1920 while serving a 10-year term for violating the Espionage Act with pacifist speeches near the end of World War I, and Meeman interviewed him for the Newspaper Enterprise Association, a Scripp-Howard subsidiary, while he was behind bars. (Debs' sentence was commuted by President Harding in 1921 after he had served three years; he died in 1926.)

When Meeman joined the Socialist Party soon after becoming a reporter for the *Evansville Press*, he was convinced that his crusty, conservative editor, F. Romer Peters, whom he later called "the greatest influence in my life," would fire him. Instead, Peters fixed him with a piercing stare and declared: "If you can stand it, we can." (Both Peters and Meeman were to die before Peters' son, Billy, a middle-aged widower formerly married to architect Frank Lloyd Wright's daughter, married Joseph Stalin's daughter, Svetlana, and, in 1971, became the father of the late dictator's granddaughter.)

Meeman was also powerfully influenced by women— Mary Baker Eddy, whom he considered the greatest woman who ever lived; Mary Collson of Evansville, Mary Allison Kimball of Knoxville, Socialist editor Florence Wattles, and others—but he never married, though he had a romance in Miami Beach in 1928–29 which he thought might have led to marriage. After their mother died in 1928, he provided a home for his sister Gertrude and his crippled brother Ben in Knoxville and Memphis for as long as they lived. They lived together amicably but without overt show of affection. When Miss Gertrude died, he searched through his files until he found a letter he had written to her from England with the words "I love you" in it, underlined them and penned in the margin: "I DID tell her."

In the dusty, yellowed papers he left as the printed record of his life, I also found memos of interest-free loans he made to countless friends and acquaintances, black and white, and records of an interest-free loan fund he established anonymously through a city welfare agency. He didn't really expect to get most of the money back; he just believed that loans fostered responsibility and preserved human dignity. There were both gifts and loans over the years to a capable but alcoholic columnist who once worked for him, and there were many outright gifts of money for special purposes, often accompanied by warm, personal notes like this one to a young student of his acquaintance: "I think you need a warmer overcoat, and I am afraid you are economizing to save money for your education.

Enclosed is a check for $100. Please buy a warm coat out of this
and put what is left in your fund for general educational expenses. . . . I certainly enjoyed my visit with you. I was delighted to see that you have a firm grip on your life and its
problems and are preparing a good future for yourself."

Other books could, and I hope will, be compiled out of the
files from which I fashioned this autobiographical collage, and
which the Edward J. Meeman Foundation has turned over to
Memphis State University. A collection of his staff memos,
forged in the blast of daily deadlines and hammered out on the
anvil of professional pride and responsibility, would provide an
invaluable text for the nation's journalism schools which, incidentally, he didn't believe in; he thought the proper training of
journalists was on the job, under the guidance of active editors.
His letters, to associates, subscribers, friends and world leaders would impress aspiring editors with how much work can,
and must, be done outside the columns of the newspaper itself
by anyone who wishes to be worthy of that title. They would
also reveal fascinating facets of human personality embodied in
one of the most extraordinary men I have ever known.

The article and series of letters he wrote in 1964 and 1965
calling for American withdrawal from Vietnam reveal how his
ideas often ran far ahead of public and official opinion, and how
diligent he was in pushing for ideas in which he believed. In
November, 1964—five years before the young people's Peace
Moratorium and almost seven years before the Pentagon
Papers—Meeman wrote his open memorandum to President
Johnson urging the immediate withdrawal of all American
troops from Vietnam. He didn't stop there. Although his feel-
ings were at odds with Scripps-Howard Newspapers' editorial
policy at the time, he asked the concern's then editor-in-chief,
Walker Stone, to make available to all its newspapers for publication his statement of dissent from the policy. Meeman was
held in such high esteem by Scripps-Howard management that
Stone acceded to his request, and most of the papers printed
the statement in full, just as I am reproducing it here:

Get out—Strengthen NATO Instead, Editor Urges
AN OPEN MEMO TO LBJ ON VIETNAM

*(THIS ARTICLE was originally a memorandum that Mr.
Meeman sent to the President on Nov. 25, 1964. Mr.
Meeman is Conservation Editor of The Scripps-Howard
Newspapers, but this article is not an expression of
Scripps-Howard, but of his own opinions.–Editors.)*

The time has come for a sharp reorientation of the position
of the U.S. in world affairs. Only if this is done can the right
decision be reached on the immediate pressing question of Vietnam.

The Past: Its Lessons

After the disillusionment of the American people with the
outcome of their "crusade for democracy" in their participation
in World War I, there was a strong determination "never again"
to be sucked into such a one. We had a policy of neutrality. But
we could not be isolated from world affairs. The only question
was HOW we would participate, how we would use our
strength.

There are a few historians, though only a few, who think
that Woodrow Wilson in his policy of "Peace without Victory"
was right the first time, that if the American people and their
President hadn't got mad when the Germans sank a munitions
ship that was also carrying passengers, who had been warned to
stay off it, the giants, Germany and Britain, would have been
forced to make a negotiated peace instead of the dictated one of
imbalance which led to the superior position of Soviet Russia on
the continent of Europe.

There are many historians who think we were starry-eyed
not to recognize that in World War II we were confronted by
two enemies, Nazi Germany and Soviet Russia, and that if we
had waged this war with realism, we would not have been
confronted with the disastrous peace that emerged with Eastern
Europe enslaved; that we should have recognized the fundamental fact that the first people to be conquered by Hitler were
the German people; the first to be enslaved by Communism
were the Russian people. We should have made a more effective
effort during World War II than we did to appeal to the good
Germans whom we now find there and who were there all the

time. Instead we cried "Unconditional Surrender" and thus solidified the German people.

Even now our hope is to make allies of the Russian people, as, since the war, we have made allies of the German people. Did you see the German people greeting Kennedy? They recognized more enthusiastically than did the American people of the time, Kennedy's greatness as the leader of the free world— their leader as well as ours. After the Russian people, we must win the wonderful Chinese people.

The United Nations was formed under an illusion—that the only problem was to keep Germany and Japan from starting another war! A deeper look would have punctured that illusion.

When we saw that the new danger was from Soviet Russia, NATO was formed. That was realism.

When, after World War II, we stood as the only great economic and military power in the world, we assumed responsibility. We were right with the Marshall Plan that put Europe on its feet. We were right to guarantee nations from aggression all over the world. Harry Truman was courageously realistic with his historic guarantees to Greece and Turkey when Britain courageously admitted she no longer was strong enough to continue them.

We now come to the time when the same kind of courageous realism requires us to face the present day facts.

If they are faced, a drastic re-orientation of U.S. policy will be indicated.

The Present: The Unrecognized Danger

The immediate need is to decide what to do about Vietnam.

That can't be decided rightly except as it is put in its place in the overall picture of world policy.

If it is assumed that the overall policy is right, a fatal mistake may be made.

For this is the first fact to be faced: The U.S. cannot continue its current willingness to protect freedom "anywhere in the world" by action on its own when the purpose is to protect the interests of all nations, and not our particular interest. We are not strong enough. We could do this after the destruction of World War II when we alone had great economic and military strength. Now economic and military strength is everywhere. Now we can no more defend world freedom alone than Britain could continue to defend Greece and Turkey when she courageously and wisely admitted she couldn't.

If we continue to let other free and independent nations think that we can, and continue to act on our own in the interest of world freedom, they surely will let us alone to try it.

We will be confronted with a new isolation—far more dangerous than the old.

The new isolation will come when quixotic Uncle Sam becomes embroiled in his own private war with Red China, and the other nations say, "Let you and him fight," The U.S. will be isolated—out on a limb.

The only way to avoid this is not to sink deeper in the Vietnam morass but to get out. When you start to sink in a swamp, the thing to do is get out before you sink over your head. Get out!

It is obvious that we can't win in Vietnam unless there is a drastic change in the Vietnamese people, unless they can quickly find unity and determination to defend their own freedom. The idea that we can win a "victory" for them and then all will be well is quixotic.

Unless the Vietnamese people change, the divisons and irresponsibility will be worse after "victory." Girls are told they shouldn't marry a man in the hope of reforming him, and we shouldn't link our lives to the Vietnamese in the hope that they will be more patriotic and see the danger of Communism more clearly than they do now. We would have to occupy the country permanently and police it, operate a military dictatorship— impossible!

A mistake does not become less of a mistake if you continue in it. If you get on the wrong road, the longer you stay on it the farther you are from where you want to go. Turn back to the crossroads where you went wrong, and get on the right road.

In the early days of Communism, the relative strength of Communism and Freedom might be measured by the amount of territory occupied by them respectively. Not now, conditions have changed. Eastern Europe, technically Communist, is militarily unreliable.

It is said our prestige will suffer if we give up in Vietnam. Not as badly as if we pursue an impossible adventure to its bitter, bitter end, when more than our prestige will suffer.

If we want to go on our own to restore freedom anywhere, the logical place to start would be Cuba. Russia is much less likely to interfere there than Red China in Vietnam. But we know the many reasons why most people think it is better to avoid action on our own even in Cuba.

We play into the hands of Red propaganda when we play the role of solitary knight.

Do now what we should have done in the first place—strengthen NATO, make it a real Atlantic Union, and put sense into the U.N. Do first things first for a while. Here is where the President's unique great persuasive powers could make great history.

If we do that, time is on our side. Mao will not last long. When he goes, Communism even in China may be very different, as it already had become different in Eastern Europe.

But if we get involved in a lone, long war far from home with the Red giant, what hope is there for our country?

But Meeman didn't stop with getting his ideas on Vietnam before Scripps-Howard readers, either.

He wrote a similar article for *Freedom & Union Magazine*, and sent clippings of both articles with covering letters to a number of U.S. leaders, including Arthur Goldberg, then U.S. ambassador to the United Nations. To Goldberg, Meeman wrote, in part:

" . . . Some of our editors chose to print (the Vietnam article), some did not. Each of them was exercising the privilege, which I enjoyed for many years, to decide what shall go in the paper for which he is responsible, and what shall not. It is a proud tradition of our papers that no editor has ever been ordered to print, or not to print, a particular piece of copy. . . .

" 'A liberal is one who realizes he may be wrong.' I accept this definition, and have tried to live up to it, though I admit I find it difficult. So I realize I may be wrong in this dissenting opinion. At the moment of writing this letter, the news from Vietnam is better. I hope it will continue to improve, and that I will be proved wrong in the fears I express in the enclosed.

"On the other hand, events may show that the present majority opinion is wrong. Majorities sometimes are. . . ."

In the voluminous files I searched to compile this book, I of course found letters to, as well as by, Meeman. One of the most moving and pertinent, in its estimate of the character and

contributions of Meeman, was written by Memphis attorney Lucius E. Burch, Jr., one of those seven men whom Meeman credited with smashing the Crump machine and sending Estes Kefauver to the Senate in the 1948 elections. On December 22, 1949, Burch wrote Meeman this letter:

Dear Ed:

As Christmas comes around and the new year approaches, I am not content with sending you a Christmas card or letting the season pass with the usual amenities. Instead, it furnishes me a reason or an excuse for telling you how grateful I am for the good influence you have had on me and for the inspiration and encouragement which you have provided, both by precept and example.

As I conduct an inner-self examination, which I do from time to time, and consider those things in my life which to me seem good and commendable, I find that a great many of the principal items would not have been but for you. You have an ability, which I have never seen approached in others, to stimulate and influence people to do good. I know several men, whose names I will not call, who, I feel, are basically egoists, self-seekers or of small vision or ability, yet these men have come under your influence and have been inspired to do great works, while other men, better endowed and constituted but lacking the stimulation of your influence, have wasted their talents. I am aware that, when you cannot persuade, you sometimes scheme to contrive artificial situations where a man must either prove himself or give up, and you sometimes appeal to weakness such as vanity, but I regard this as legitimate for it proceeds from sound and honorable motives.

In the substantial accomplishments of recent years, such as a quickened public interest in such things as the Atlantic Union Committee, the Citizens Committee, the Civic Research Committee and in the effecting of a decent and humane relationship between employer and employee, between responsible white citizens and responsible Negro citizens, there is everywhere your handiwork and your effect upon it all has been causal in the sense, that, but for you, it would not have been.

You do not need these assurances and I suspect that you get little pleasure from them. It gives me pleasure to express them, however, in an effort to lessen the burden of the debt by

acknowledging it and also because I value your good opinion
enough to want you to know *that I know the origin of all this
good, much of which will be recorded and remembered in connection with the names of other men.*

I hope during the coming year and for many years the Lord
will keep and protect you and make His face to shine upon you,
for the reflection from you is felt by many who have neither as
great nor as direct access to this source of spiritual strength.

With compliments of the season and every good wish for
you and yours, I remain,

Sincerely your friend,
Lucius E. Burch

Less encyclopedic in content and perhaps less felicitous in
expression, but no less heart-felt and deserved, this brief undated note from a staff member to the editor was also in his files:

EJM:
You are so good to share so many wonderful things with me.
What a joy each and every one of them are! Words won't express
my deep devotion to you and my sincere appreciation, but
please know I am grateful. Just being associated with you is one
of the richest blessings of my life.

So most of us felt who were privileged to work for and with
this great editor and man. Zollie Howard, who as reporter and
city editor in Knoxville and managing editor and associate
editor in Memphis, worked longer and more closely with him
than anyone else, began his editorial on Meeman's passing in
this way:

Mankind is like a great cable stretching from the misty past
to the misty future. All of us are strands twisted into this cable,
some long, some short; some contributing strength, some
weakness. Ed Meeman was a long, strong strand in the cable . . .
his work and the influence of his personality will be woven into
the future by the life-strands which the strand of his own life
touched. . .

George Carmack, former editor of *The Albuquerque
Tribune,* who worked for Meeman as reporter and city editor
in Memphis, wrote:" . . . I consider him one of the most re-

markable men I have ever known—certainly the most courageous man, the most deeply religious man, the man most devoted to the good of his community, his nation, his world and
his fellow man. I can think of only one man I ever knew who
could truly be called a noble man. That was Ed Meeman."

Edward J. Meeman did aspire to nobility, and achieved far
more than he knew or would admit. Like all men, he had
weaknesses, and one of the greatest of his weaknesses was the
belief, or at least the hope, that life could somehow be reduced
to some simple formula whose rightness all men would recognize and follow. Although he would not have admitted it, he
spent his life seeking such a formula. He sought it, and at times
thought he had found it, in Christian Socialism, Christian
Science, and in the Oxford Movement (later known as Moral
Re-Armament.) More than most men, he had strengths, and
the greatest of his strengths was the ability and willingness to
see his mistakes and to change his mind. It was this open-
mindedness that made him free and, in the true and literal
sense, quite apart from all the ideological barnacles the word
has accumulated in the last half-century, a liberal.

In the following pages you will learn, in Meeman's own
words, how he encountered and wrestled with these ideas and
how they motivated him in the great public services he per-
formed for the people of Indiana, Tennessee, the Mid-South,
the United States, and the world. By his own estimate, he was a
"back-country" editor in a country which had "too long rested
passive under the influences generated in the great centers of
New York and Washington." He felt it was "time that the
centers should be influenced by the back country." and more
than any editor of his time, I believe, he influenced them.

In the Meeman autobiography which I have constructed
out of his writings, there emerges a trio of basic interests and
concerns. They were the relationships between man and man,
between man and his natural environment, and between man
and God.

These were his Trinity. They motivated him throughout

the almost 60-year newspaper career which was his life, and of which this book is the record. Because it is in his own words, it is a modest record, but it is my hope that its publication may serve to lighten the burden of the debt owed to him by the millions who have been touched and benefited, most of them unknowingly, by his devotion to that Trinity.

A Note on the Compilation of This Book

The best but most fragmentary of several incomplete book manuscripts I found in the files of Edward J. Meeman when I was given access to them by the Meeman Foundation three years after his death, was one he called "My Spiritual Autobiography." Consisting of some 80 double-spaced typewritten pages full of strike-overs and write-ins, it was apparently intended as an account of his theological development. But alone with his typewriter, with no particular cause to champion, Meeman was above all a story-teller; he kept getting off the theological throughway onto delightful narrative side roads. What emerged was truly a "spiritual" autobiography rather than merely a religious one—a brief but bright, personal and incisive account of the formative influences and episodes in his life.

This manuscript, with 18 pages of heavier than lucid theological ruminations eliminated, I determined to use as the narrative line for the book. It was sketchy and incomplete, particularly in its treatment of the latter half of his life, but like the initial "treatment" of 50 pages or so for a motion picture script, it contained the plot line, all the major themes, and at least passing reference to the major events of his life.

I then determined to elaborate on that narrative line, as a contemporary motion picture scenarist might, with flashbacks, flash-forwards, and montages in the form of editorials, articles, poems, letters and speeches selected from his files. In interpolating this material, all written by Meeman, into the narrative, I sought to achieve not necessarily a chronological unity—the narrative itself provided that—but a thematic unity. As flashbacks or flash-forwards may be cued in a modern motion picture by a passing word or thought of the principal character, so in this autobiography I have introduced thematic elaborations drawn from his voluminous other writings.

The interpolations are set off from the body of the narrative by indentation and a smaller type face, and are identified as to date, place and form of their origination. (I would have preferred to set them off with different colored inks—black for the narrative, green for editorials, red for letters, blue for speeches, and so on—as William Faulkner wanted to set off the narratives of the different characters in "The Sound and the Fury." What Random House denied Faulkner, however, I lacked the nerve to ask of my publisher.)

My aim throughout was simply to find, edit and arrange those writings of Edward J. Meeman which would most readably, truthfully and effectively tell, in his own words, the story of his remarkable life and career. This, then, is his life, as he lived and wrote it.

—Edwin Howard

The Editorial We

John Henry Meeman, father of Edward J. Meeman.

1907 Graduating Class of Evansville High School (Edward J. Meeman is fourth from the left in the front row).

Edward J. Meeman (farthest back) and friends at a logging site in the Great Smoky Mountains.

Edward J. Meeman, Senator Estes Kefauver, Edmund Orgill
in June, 1951.　　　　　　Courtesy of *The Press-Scimitar*

Edward J. Meeman at home. This picture was printed on the cover of the *Scripps-Howard News* in 1955 on the occasion of the 75th anniversary of *The Press-Scimitar*. Meeman is shown on the road of his 612-acre Forest Farm.

Courtesy of *Scripps-Howard News*

The Kefauver Committee in April of 1960. Left to right: O.D. Bratton, Edmund Orgill, William M. Barr, Edward J. Meeman, Edwin A. Dalstrom, Lucius E. Burch, Jr., and Dr. Henry B. Gotten   Courtesy of *The Press-Scimitar*

Edward J. Meeman

This photograph was used as a "signature" picture for his signed
articles and columns for *The Press-Scimitar*. Courtesy of *The
Press-Scimitar*

The Edward J. Meeman Journalism Building, Memphis State University. Dedicated November 7, 1971.

I

School Days in Evansville: Early Religious and Educational Experiences—"Too Bright" for Catholic School—"God Is Like a Mountain"—Leaving the Church: "I Don't Believe in It Any More!"—Freedom

Solomon, moralist, has enjoined us to "remember the Creator in the days of thy youth," and speaks truly. But it is with equal truth that Byron, the poet, tells us that "the days of our youth are the days of our glory." The high moral precept in the first has ever been expounded to us by our elders, for they lose no opportunity to furnish us with the maxims of righteousness. But the other, which is also one of the fundamental verities of life, we have been left to discover for ourselves. The class of June, '07 has found this thought of Byron's and appropriated it for its own. It has enunciated it as a living principle and lived up to it conscientiously. Youth is often considered only as a preparation for the achievements of maturity.

But for June, '07, youth is sufficient unto itself. It is worth living for its own sweet sake.

—Edward J. Meeman, in *The High School Record*, Evansville, Indiana June, 1907

I was born in a little one-story brick house on Harriet Street in Evansville, Indiana, on October 2, 1889. I do not remember living in that house. The first thing I remember was being in the house next door, on the corner of Franklin, which was the home of my godfather, Edward Bitter, a tailor. It was a two-story brick house. Both were Roman Catholic households.

The first thing I sharply remember is being carried upstairs in that house by Mary Bitter, housekeeper for the

1

widower, Edward Bitter. I do not know why their names were the same.

On the landing, in the half light, I saw a picture of the head of Jesus, crowned with thorns, tears of agony falling from his eyes. I burst into tears of fear and anguish at the sight. I do not know whether, as a child in arms, two, three, or four years old, my memory of this is unaided, or whether I was told of it afterward. I do know it is the first experience of my life that I clearly and strongly remember.

I think it had great influence on me. I think the distress it gave me is one of the things that caused me to reject the emphasis which most of the followers of Jesus have placed on his crucifixion, his sacrifice, his death, and to stress instead his life, his teachings, his example. I do not believe that Jesus was sent into the world by God to die for us. I think his mission was that which John quotes him as saying to Pilate:

"For this I was born, and for this I have come into the world, to bear witness to the truth."

It may be that the life and words of Jesus would never have had the attention, influence, and power they have had if he had not been a martyr. If so, that is a commentary on the error in human nature, which requires sensational events to obtain its attention.

I am glad that the first choice, or the first impression, of my life was to turn away from that tragedy with distaste and revulsion. It made Jesus unhappy, and it made me unhappy to see it. Such salvation as I have found, I have found not in Jesus's death, but in his life, his great life, the greatest of all lives. I have found good in his willingness to give his life, but not in his actual death.

My second memory is of the street cars, electric trolley cars, as I looked out the window of my godfather's house and saw them clattering along Franklin Street. How wonderful I thought they were, how wonderful I still think they are. When in high school I saw my school mate and rich friend, Dyer Butterfield, riding with his grandfather in one of the first

Cadillacs in town, I thought it was wonderful, too. But I was to come to think of the automobile as a symbol of man's failure to learn how to use and live with his inventions. I first wrote "man's inability". I struck it out, as false to what I believe. I do not think man lacks any needful ability. I think, let me say I know, that man has the ability to solve all his problems. We fail because we do not use that ability. We fail to think and act with the boldness and certainty of which it has been proved we are capable. Mankind is not defective. Man does not need to be a different being than he is. Man cannot understand the Universe completely, but we can learn all we need to know.

I remember Mary Bitter cooking preserves—was it apple butter?—on the kitchen stove. As a toddler, I called it prit-prot, for that is the way it sounded, deliciously, as it gently boiled. My early childhood was a gentle prit-prot of peace and contentment. Days of life entirely among working people, mostly happy people, mostly virtuous, mostly having peace of mind. I was not to know insecurity until I became rich, for by that time everybody in the world had become insecure. That peaceful world, where all war and revolution was in the past, merely a romance to enliven the piping days of peace, failed to fulfill the great promise it held. It was shattered by more terrible war and revolution than Earth had ever seen before.

My mother was Mary Elisabeth Schulte. She was the daughter of Heinrich Schulte, a German farmer whose farm, known as Feldkamp, is near Isterkappeln, which is a village lying between Hanover and Osnabrueck. The family is said to be descended from a sea captain who settled there.

Grandfather was an idealist. He was devoted to the Queen of Hanover. My mother's brother, Francis Joseph Schulte, who became a book publisher in Chicago, told me that the Queen had Grandfather's picture, in soldier's uniform, in the palace, as typical of her subjects. That may have been the reason for his fanatical devotion to the royal family. There is a vague, very vague, legend in the family of some connection, probably left-handed, between my mother's family and the royal Hanoverians. Be that as it may, my grandfather, my mother told me, was so devoted to the Queen that when she was deposed by the absorption of Hanover by the Kaiser, he did not want to live there any longer, and decided to leave the country for America. Here a second phase of his idealism was manifested. He sold the family farm to a Catholic for much less than he could have got from a Protestant, because he did not want to reduce the number of Catholics in the parish. Grandfather and his wife and eight children crossed the Atlantic in a sailing vessel. One child died at sea. They went to St. Louis, where grandfather invested the proceeds of the sale of the farm in a boarding house. It failed. But the older children went to work and they made out.

My father, John Henry Meeman, was the son of a huckster, who bought vegetables from the farmers and sold them to the city people of St. Louis. John fell in love with the sweet and beautiful Mary Elisabeth Schulte. He quoted Byron to her. He told her if she would not marry him he would kill himself. She believed him. Her tender heart was moved and she married him. She did not love him; she never learned to love him.

My father became a periodical drinker. He would come home drunk and sit there and say: "Nobody cares for me." Mother and we children would not deny it. "How can we love you when you behave like this?" True, nobody loved him, except his fellow workers in the cigar shop, where his fingers, the most skilled in the shop, made the finest and most expensive of Havanas; he was such a good worker that the proprietor was always willing to take him back after each spree.

My father's fellow workers saw in him the qualities I did not appreciate until after he had gone—his wisdom, his thoughtfulness. If only there had been someone to teach my mother how to deal with him, someone to tell us children that he never "disgraced" us, as we thought, even when he fell in the gutter and was brought home and laid upon a bed, unable to walk. We did not know that no one can bring disgrace upon one but oneself. The kindly neighbors understood, never condemned, but sympathized. But we never understood; we heaped our righteous condemnation upon Papa until it was too late.

Now I know what I owe him. I remember, as we all sat around the big walnut dining room table in the evening, mother sewing, the children getting their lessons, him reading the newspaper thoroughly and looking up from it to make his sage comments. I remember how he would go to the "Little Market", actually a big market, in the square in Evansville. The farmers would drive their wagons into the middle of the square, and back them up to stands next to the sidewalks. The stands would be open into the night, gas lamps furnishing the light, making a glamorous sight—horses, wagons, the red-checked shirts of German farmers, neat, fresh, crisp, bright vegetables. We would make one trip around the square, taking a look at every stand and asking prices. Then we would go a second time and buy. My father carried a flour sack, filled it full of the delicious bargains, swung it over his shoulder and then we would take the electric street car (tram car) for home. Sometimes he would go alone; always he would come home with a sackful. He not only bought vegetables; he raised them. Our backyard yielded all summer long. How much of my good health I owe to my father's appreciation of the value of vegetables! He would not compel us to eat them, but he would sing praises of their deliciousness—"these turnips make blood"—so that we wanted to eat them.

My home was not a place of misery; I had many happy times there. But on the whole it could not be called a happy home because my mother did not return the love my father gave her, and he turned to drink. So school was a refuge from my home, as work was later to be. There I found in my teachers higher standards of thinking, feeling, behavior, taste and manners than I found at home. There my precocity won me respect from both teachers and fellow students as a "smart boy." No one seemed to think less of me because I was not very proficient in games; there was tacit recognition that a smart boy

shouldn't be expected to be good at games, too, and I was
allowed to enjoy playing at them though never playing well. I
can remember almost nothing but enlightenment, kindness
and love in all my twelve years at school. The exceptions are so
slight that they seem next to nothing now, though they seemed
something at the time.

When I was eight years old a teacher got tired of my
restless squirming, threw me over her lap, face toward the
floor, to keep me quiet while she held her book above my body
and conducted the lesson. She was not unkind, she meant no
harm, but I felt deeply humiliated. In that same year, I was
stuffing a lot of paper in a wastebasket and in doing so, dropped
to my knees. My chum, Walter Spear—we were the best of
friends and became lifelong friends—came in at that moment,
said "Ed is praying to the trash basket!" and spread the word
over the school. Probably no one took this seriously but me; I
suffered terribly over it. I thought they believed it.

Once a big boy bullied me a little—so little that I cannot
remember what the incident was. He died suddenly when we
were in the seventh grade, the only member of my grammar
school class to die in all the eight years. I was grieved; also I felt
the tragedy—how are the mighty fallen.

How I came to be a pupil in the free public taxpayer-
supported school is part of a wonderful story. My mother was a
nominal Roman Catholic. She was not of a religious temperament. Her life was motivated by her sense of duty. She went to
church for the same reason that she kept her children well fed,
well scrubbed, and well clothed. She was delighted when
washday came. She never tired. "Let me do it" she would often
say when one of us children sought to do some little task. She
also knew it was expected of her by her brothers and sisters, all
of whom were devoted Catholics except her youngest brother,
Joe, who became a Presbyterian. At the time, this defection
was attributed to his wife, Kate, whom he met when both were
proofreaders on the St. Louis *Post-Dispatch*.

My father had been an altar boy, brought up by a strict

Catholic mother. Her extreme strictness was a legend. Was that one of the reasons why my father had become an agnostic before I was born? He went so far in deriding religion that when sitting at the table, he would mockingly make the sign of the cross as the priest does when blessing the congregation. He would solemnly chant *"Dominus vobiscum."* Since we did not think much of our father, this did not prejudice us against Catholicism; on the contrary, we esteemed it more because he made fun of it. "Papa, don't do that," we would say. But we didn't mind it very much—we may even have been amused.

But my father was tolerant. He allowed my mother to send my older brother and two sisters to the Catholic schools. They were German immigrant schools, and unenlightened. My brother and sisters were unhappy there. One sister, Gertrude, told of a teacher hitting the children on the palm with a ruler. She told of a terrifying sermon she heard at St. Anthony's church. Father Schutt gave this picture of Hell: In it was a pendulum swinging forever, never stopping. The pendulum swung from one point to another. "Immer—Nimmer." "Forever—Never." Gertrude was terrified by this picture. Later in life she had no religious faith at all. I was to learn that these backward schools were the exception; that many Catholic schools are enlightened in educational standards and methods.

But this was the kind of school to which I would have gone if I had been sent to the Catholic school. The family were unanimous that I should be spared that experience: "Eddie is too bright a boy for that." So they hid me from the priest. When the priest made a pastoral call, I was not included in the list of children they gave him; he never knew I existed. However, it was a large church, a large congregation, and I would often go to mass, slipping into one of the unpaid pews on the side at the back, where I was never noticed.

Ironically, I was of a religious temperament and craved the instructions I was being denied. My father, again broadminded, took me to the priest at the English-speaking Irish church downtown, and arranged with him to instruct me in the catechism after public school hours. I understood he made a contribution to pay for this.

I eagerly drank in what Father McBarron gave me. I thought to myself that I was more interested in learning than he was in instructing me. The great historic church and its religion enthralled me. I remember that one day I dropped to my knees, raised my eyes to heaven and vowed to restore the church to its former glory. I was confirmed; I remember the solemn moment when the bishop, in mitered cap, put the holy oil on my forehead and muttered the Latin words. I remember the sense of purity, the unearthly taste of the wafer, as I took my first communion. I was in effect a convert to Catholicism at the age of 12, for my home had imposed little religion on me. I was a good Catholic. How I loved to go to high mass, to follow its beautiful progression: the sprinkling of the congregation with holy water by the young priest, Father Ryves, as he walked down the aisle with handsome, uplifted head, the magnificent strains of *Kyrie Eleison* ("Lord have mercy on us") and the *Gloria in Excelsis* ("Glory to God in the highest") coming from the loft in the rear of the church. The singers were remote and superhuman, like angels, not like ordinary human beings one could stare at, sitting behind the preacher in the little Presbyterian mission chapel which I had attended with my chum. I especially like *Dominus vobiscum* ("The Lord be with you"), and *Et cum Spiritu tuo* ("And with thy spirit"), perhaps because my father had mocked it.

I liked the swinging censers, and their fragrance that filled the great church. I liked the beautiful marble statue of the Virgin. I liked the stained glass.

I felt the solemnity of the moment when the bell rang, and the bread became the body of Christ. But unabashed and curious, I would lift my bowed head to look at the Host in its golden container, and at another time, I would look backward to steal a glance at the angel choir in the loft above.

How fondly I remember Lent! It was not a time of sacrifice for us, but of enjoyment. My agnostic father cared nothing about the religious part. Just as in the fall he made a great jar of sauerkraut for the winter ("It's good for you," he said, and no doubt, with the absence of fresh vegetables, it was), so he pickled herring, delicious with onions and spices, for Lent.

I have long supposed that the superstitious warning, "It's unlucky to walk under a ladder," was a parent's shorthand for the longer explanation: "If you walk under a ladder, something may fall on you from those working on it above you, and you may get hurt." So I have believed that the injunction, "It's a sin to eat meat on Fridays or on fast days," is a similar corruption of the wise order of some early church father, who saw that it was good for nutrition, and economical, to vary the diet and eat fish, which is always wholesome and, if it comes from the sea, contains all the minerals which may be missing from food grown on land.

How fondly I remember those evenings, sometimes warm with an early spring, when with the delicious taste of herring and onions lingering on my palate, I walked the mile or so to church with my sisters. Yes, walked! Concrete, hated change which was not progress, was just coming in. Most of the sidewalks were of brick, delightful to walk upon. There was no traffic to disturb or menace.

How solemn and dramatic was the observance of the Way of the Cross. At intervals along the walls of the church there were paintings, each representing some incident in the tragic procession to Calvary. At each the priest and his servitors would kneel and intone prayers, the choir singing as they moved from station to station. I will never forget the words of Father Ryves:

"Grant that I may love Thee always, and then do with me what Thou wilt!"

I was deeply moved by those words, but not deeply enough. If I had committed myself to them wholly and utterly, if I had given up all will of my own, and known no will but God's, my life would have been wholly a success, instead of only partially a success. Slowly, gradually, I have yielded to the will of God. But not wholly. Almost. To surrender utterly to God, but unyielding to the powers and blandishments of the world—that is true religion, and it can be found in more than one faith.

(Signed editorial from The Memphis Press-Scimitar, February 19, 1962.)

"GOD IS LIKE A MOUNTAIN"

"Why are there so many religions?" asks the skeptic. "They can't all be true, so I don't think any of them are true."

To the skeptic I answer:

There are many roads to the mountain, from many directions.

From some of the roads, those traveling see the mountain first in the dim distance, gradually growing clearer.

From others, the travelers come to a turn in their journey and suddenly the mountain bursts on their view, entire and complete, breathtaking and awesome.

There are many vantage points from which the mountain can be seen.

Some see him from the far end of the valley, some from the very foot.

Some see him from the adjoining peak of high philosophy. Some see him as they till the busy lowlands of service. Some see him from the picnic grounds of joy in living. Some see him from a simple cottage; some from a many-roomed mansion. Some see him from a great distance, others near at hand. Some see him only by a passing glance in the swift flight of an airplane as they hurry about their worldly affairs.

Some come deluxe by automobile.

Some, in walking boots and with knapsack, come by foot, loving every step of the way, their appetite for the close-up sharpened by the rugged journey.

These climb the mountain, and learn the form and nature of every herb and bush and tree that graces his surface, the fragrance of every flower, the breath of every wind, the flavor of every berry, fruit and nut, the song of every bird, the cry and ways of every beast the great mountain bears in his bosom. Some cling to the lower slopes, some climb all the way to the pure snows of the very summit.

Some come to the mountain in an organized group, captained by a trustworthy and confident leader, with experienced guides, lest they become lost. What joy to see the smile of assurance in the leader's eyes! Others think they can find their way in twos and threes. A few make the journey all alone, one by one, and some of these, too, find the glory.

The approaches are different. The viewpoints are different. The knowledge of the mountain varies in intimacy, fullness, depth and height. The experiences of those who come to the mountain are different.

But the mountain is ever the same, always there to be learned, to challenge with his difficulty, to be explored, to be revered, to inspire with his majesty and beauty.

The different ways and approaches are our different religions. The different viewpoints are our different theologies.

Who shall say that only one road leads to the mountain? Who shall say that only one view of the mountain is true, that he can be seen from only one spot?

But ah! It is quite another thing to believe and say that the road you have traveled is best, to call to others to join you on it. This we may do. It is all right to say: "I know where there is a wonderful view of the mountain, come with me and I will show you." It is all right to say: "I can tell you where the flowers are brightest, where the blueberries are thickest and most luscious, where the stream is cold and clear and the waterfall spills melodiously into deep pools and the fish bite—where there are blessings and pleasures forevermore." Of course, love prompts us to do that.

The mountain is always the same, always there, belonging to all of us in common, however we come to him, and however he may look at us—limitless in beauty, variety and richness for us to worship and enjoy.

Of course, we all see what is in the foreground of our particular landscape. We should not tell the other man he does not see what he says he sees in his foreground. That foreground is our particular theology and creed. We look through it and past it, all of it, to the same mountain, to the same central Reality.

Love our mountain, love all who have found him, love all who seek him, by whatever road they take. Love even those who have not heard his call to them to come.

I remember, too, going on sunny Sunday afternoons to

vespers, and hearing the Psalms sung in Latin, which seemed like a veritable mother tongue to me from the moment I first heard it.

If I now see inadequacy in this youthful spiritual experience, nevertheless it was genuine, real and meaningful.

But there was another process going on—my education in the wonderful schools of Indiana.

All my teachers were enlightened and kind. There was the tall, beautiful gray-haired mother, Mrs. Mary White, my first-grade teacher, in the old building at Baker school, with its high ceilings and heavy walnut doorways. Our rich age, poverty-stricken in its soul, thinks it cannot afford them now. The outdoor urinal, with its rusty tin trough, smelled—but what of that? Open to the air, winter and summer, it wasn't a bad smell. Our old building had dignity and beauty, and so did the teaching that went on inside.

Our fourth grade teacher wore glasses, and did not look very happy and we said: "She is a cross old maid." But it was this Miss Durham, who, at her own expense, took the whole class to Garvin's woods for a Saturday picnic, with a treat, fresh strawberries and ice cream, which few of us ever had had at home.

In the sixth grade the gentle Miss Bertha Lockwood read the 23rd Psalm every day, without comment. In later years I was to learn that she was a Christian Scientist.

In the eighth grade, under the direction of Miss Weber, we pupils bought a magnificent reproduction of the *Aurora*, by Guido Reni, which was my introduction to "the glory that was Greece and the grandeur that was Rome." I was chosen to tell the story of the painting to the class and to a teacher's meeting. The words *"Castle Rospigliosi"* tripped off my agile tongue so nimbly that they laughed, not in ridicule, but in admiration.

Magnificent pedagogy—Miss Weber had every one of us learn "by heart," at the age of 12 or less, Shelley's "To a Skylark"—

Hail to thee blithe spirit!...

Teach me half the gladness
That thy brain must know,
Such harmonious madness
From my lips would flow,
The world should listen then, as I am listening now.

Learning that poem "by heart", and reciting it before the class, made me an appreciator and lover of Shelley, and of all English poetry.

(From The High School Record, Evansville, Indiana, 1906)

A Sonnet

Of my eventless days my chafed soul doth cry,
"How hard the lot to which I must submit,
Condemned to love the world, yet never taste of it,
And lead a life of dull obscurity.
For the world's stirring life must I forever sigh,
And in a studious corner always sit,
To read the books that other men have writ?"
Yet as I speak an inner voice doth thus reply:
"Complain not vainly thus of heaven's will,
All will be well if thou but trust thy worth,
In later years thou shalt obtain thy crown.
But now rest thou in patient peace until
The trump of high events shall call thee forth
To battle, and to deeds of great renown."

—Edward Meeman

Later I was to read in Maurice Hewlett's "Open Country," how we got the phrase "by heart". People loved poetry so much that they could not forget it, but knew every word. With us pupils, it was a reverse process, we were ordered to memorize the words. This made us so familiar with them that we could not escape their beauty and meaning, and so they remained in our hearts.

Learning "To a Skylark" by heart lifted my life to a higher level. How can we adequately value a teacher who will give us such an experience!

There were many such teachers in the Evansville High School. Thanks to them I got the foundation which with supplementary reading I did during and after school days, thanks to the love of learning they instilled, gave me what I have felt was the equivalent of a college education. It was no soft course: four years of English, including English and American literature; four years of Latin, a year of French, three years of mathematics, a year of biology, one year of Physics, four years of history, ancient, medieval, modern and American; a year of typewriting, and shorthand.

Miss Mary Armstrong and Miss Ella Bourne, dedicated teachers who later went to Mt. Holyoke College, induced in us something of the great love they felt for Roman civilization and the Latin language. Miss Daisy Flower, daughter of the New England editor of *Arena Magazine*, B.O Flower, taught us not only love of English literature and kept us from being infected with the vestiges of Victorian prudery which remained after the turn of the century, but prepared us to be secure from the assault of literary filth that was to come.

(Signed editorial from the Memphis Press-Scimitar, January 23, 1952.)

I was delighted on a recent Sunday to see so many people enjoying Shelby Forest though the calendar said it was January.

When I first moved to the country people asked: "Do you stay out there all year?" When I answered yes I would often add that I like the country just as well in winter as summer. Then I reflected on why that was so.

I recalled one day in the second grade of high school when my English teacher, Daisy Flower, put on the blackboard a suggested list of subjects on which we might write compositions. One of them was "The Bare Tree."

That was an awakening to me. Until that moment I had thought of nature in winter as empty, merely a time of waiting for spring to return. That winter should have any beauty of its own had not occurred to me. But I saw it then, and I have seen it ever since. From the time Miss Flower wrote the words "The Bare Tree" on the board, I have seen beauty in every winter-sleeping tree.

No tree in its summer green could be more beautiful than the white-trunked sycamore on the Walsh road which I see frequently when I take that route to town.

What a debt we owe to our teachers! I learned from Daisy Flower not only to love the great English tongue, and to read its best, and to write my best, but much besides. She was the daughter of B.O. Flower, editor of the *Arena*, a New England magazine which carried no advertising, but which, I believed, by its unconventionality, had a good influence on the late Victorian era, which ended in 1914, when it was published. Miss Flower taught us that to be unkind was not the way to uphold virtue. She looked up from "David Copperfield" to exclaim against the terrible shock that everybody registered when Emily was betrayed by Steerforth, and how a little more casualness would have been more considerate. Later another great English teacher, William Lyon Phelps, quoted Ben Franklin: "A civilized man is one who is never shocked at anything." In those days any woman over 25 was deemed an "old maid," especially if she wore glasses, so we students were much surprised when she married her high school sweetheart, although they had drifted apart after school days. I haven't a doubt that she "managed" the reunion. They lived happily ever after.

And how poor my life would have been without the philanthropy of Willard Carpenter! He had built the Willard library, sitting in a green part opposite Market Square, a Byzantine building filled with all the great books and some good stories, too. As a boy, I read mostly stories—in vacation time, sometimes six books a week. I read every one of the G.A. Henty stories. Henty, an Englishman, wrote a book about a boy's adventures in nearly every one of England's wars, crises and enterprises. This was a preparation for later reading of English history and literature, which was to make me think of England as a second motherland. Germany also became a second motherland.

In my late grammar school and early high school years, I

read deeply and widely. I took on such heavy tomes as Mommsen's *History of Rome* and the seven volumes of Guizot's history of France.

(Walter Spear's 1907 Class Prophecy, in the form of a 1937 class reunion report, from The High School Record, Evansville, Indiana.)

... Edward Meeman, a small, intelligent-looking man, got up at one of the tables and, after clearing his throat, began:

"Classmates, I have little to show for the thirty years gone by. The reason for this is that I had too much talent. When I graduated, I was a poet, a linguist, a scientist, and a number of other things. With such a variety of accomplishments, I was at a loss what to do. I finally began teaching a country school, but as this was not congenial, I resigned and took up a position on the Newburg *Liberalist*. I succeeded so well that I went to that city of eternal promise, New York. Here I advanced rapidly in my profession and was beginning to make a name for myself when the French Revolution of 1919 broke out. Eager to be of service to this then loved country, I hastened to Paris, but I was run ignominiously out of the country. I returned to the United States and began writing "The Fall of the French," a work which had I finished, would have taken the world by storm. But when I was about half through it I became interested in some discoveries which were then being made about evolution. And so it has been. Various talents struggling for mastery in me had made a failure, while others have reaped the benefit of my years of work. I have never married for some reason. In my younger days, I never met a girl that I thought was quite worthy of EDWARD MEEMAN. Of late, I have been benefitted by my experiences and I am now editing the *International*, and have a chair in Harvard University. The time will come when—"

"Time's up," interrupted Mr. Young and Mr. Meeman took his seat amid the applause of his classmates and spectators. They were all puzzled to know what Mr. Meeman meant by his being "a failure," for he was considered one of the greatest successes of the day. They did not know that he meant internal failure, the realization of the fact that he had fallen short of the ideal of his High School Days.

As a young adolescent, as I have said, I was a devout Catholic. But questions arose even while I was taking my instructions in the catechism.

Apparently it was the custom of the priests to get together occasionally at one of the rectories at the end of the day, and a group came into the Assumption rectory one day just as my lesson was finishing. In my reading I had come upon a discussion of Arius and his heresy of the Fourth Century, and had asked Father McBarron about it. Father McBarron clapped me on the back and said to the priests with a laugh, "This lad wants to know about Arianism!" I thought I was being ridiculed; I thought my interest in theology should be encouraged and satisfied. Perhaps I was oversensitive, but I did not like it.

I continued my reading of history. I read of the bishops and popes, of their struggles for power, of their ambitions, their intrigues, their mistresses.

At last I faced what I had come to think.

"Why, the Roman church is not divine, its pope is not infallible—this is a human institution!"

The movement of my mind to this conclusion had been aided by an experience in the confessional. I smelled liquor on the priest's breath. Perhaps I was prudish, but it didn't seem right to me.

I kept what was going on in my mind and heart to myself. I feared to tell my mother and sisters.

There came the Saturday in spring when I would have to go to confession so as to be able to receive communion the next day, or be automatically excommunicated from the church.

"Eddie, why aren't you taking your bath so you can go to confession?"

I burst into tears and ran upstairs to my room. A few minutes later I came down and cried out, in the presence of my sisters:

"Mama, I can't go. I don't believe in it any more!"

I expected to be upbraided. Instead, my sister Gertrude said:

"Oh that's all right—Cousin Will has left the church, too!"

That was Will Westerman, who had shown us the St. Louis World's Fair and we greatly admired him.

Oh, the joyous relief I felt. I was free.

My mother was somewhat concerned about what the relatives would think—that was all. Many of our family had gone into religious orders. On my study wall today hangs a picture of the Bishop of Osnabrueck in Germany, my great-great-uncle on my mother's side.

The whole family followed me out of the church. I had been the one who held them to their religious duties. I was the one in the family most interested in religion. When I ceased to believe, when I relaxed the pressure, they no longer went to mass.

I would not give up my spiritual experience in the Catholic church. I feel that I have retained what I found true, beautiful and good in the great old church.

I relived that experience in 1955 in Mainz, when on a summer morning, before embarking for my Rhine journey to Cologne, I entered the ancient Cathedral. I dropped to my knees in an ecstasy of devotion to the God of that church and all churches, feeling at one with all the worshippers in all the centuries who had sought and found their God and my God in that holy place, dedicating myself to the Christ—the spirit of Truth, Love and healing Power of that church and of all mankind.

II

Graduation and First Job: $4-a-Week
Reporter—Atheism: Contracted and
Cured—Introduction to Christian Science

Like most members of my high school class, Dyer Butterfield, at least at the time, admired my precocity. He was the
son of the leading bookseller, the grandson of the wealthy
lawyer, Azro Dyer. One day I got this note, in a boyish pen-
ciled scrawl on stationery embossed in bright blue letters:

"I am at home with a hole in my head. Won't you come and
spend the day with me?"

It was my first experience of how wealthy people lived.
The Butterfield house was on South First Street, on the corner
of Oak, the best residence street. It was a square brick house,
with a wide hall running down the center. The hardwood floors
gleamed. Luncheon was a revelation to me. The bearded Mr.
Butterfield came home for it, as was the custom of business
men in small cities. The conversation flowed easily and pleas-
antly. The Butterfields treated each other as politely as they
would strangers. That was not so at our house. Our food was
always good, but a meal was an occasion without grace, often
marred by bickering and arguments which were almost quar-
rels.

After lunch Mrs. Butterfield went to the sideboard,
picked up a dish of hard candy and passed it. Candy sitting out
where anyone could get it! At our house we seldom had candy
except at Christmas or when we paid our grocery bill on

Saturdays and the grocer gave us a sack as lagniappe, which was divided among the children and immediately consumed.

It was the first of many happy visits to the homes of the rich, the well-born, the cultivated. I always felt at home in them, as if it were the lift I was meant for. I always intensely enjoyed what they shared with me, and vicariously, entirely without envy, the part they did not share. When I attained to wealth and a beautiful home of my own, I reflected that I could not have enjoyed them as much as I did, if I had not been able to enjoy vicariously the possessions of others.

(From the High School Record, Evansville, Indiana, 1906)

MY CASTLE IN SPAIN

We all have our castle in Spain, but who can accurately describe his? Universal law decrees that they shall be bright, gay, impossibly majestic, and ephemeral.

My castles are so vague that they may be embellished at each describing of them without exactly telling a falsehood, until the superstructure becomes too heavy for the foundation and down topple the spires, walls, sculptures and even the foundation itself. But the stores of the imagination are infinite and another structure is built upon the ruins of its predecessor, not so filled with untasty, gaudy ornamentation, but grander in its proportions and materials.

This one exists longer, and so on, the evolution continues, building more substantial edifices out of the old, till at last there may be a simple house filled with realities, not built of the imagination, but of the mind, with a threshold that may be crossed and floors upon which one may tread, magnificent in its simplicity, and best of all, a possibility.

—E. Meeman, '07

If one cannot, in the words of Whitman, enjoy "without labor or purchase," he cannot enjoy fully what he has obtained with labor or purchase. Envy is indeed a deadly sin, which brings instant and continuing punishment. If only the Marxists had learned this!

Dyer took me to his church, the church of the rich, Grace

Presbyterian, a solid church of stone walls, stained glass, and fine wood interior finish. I was impressed by the learned sermons of Dr. H.A. Hymes, though they left me somewhat cold.

Sunday school was a rich experience. It was taught by Henry Walker, a leading lawyer, who had graduated from Princeton University. He showed how the Old Testament was the history of the Jewish people, their search for God, and their experience of him; that all parts of the Bible were not of equal value. I quickly saw for myself that some parts of it were not holy at all.

High school finished, I had become a reporter on the Evansville *Press*.

(From Scripps-Howard News of November, 1953)

After graduating from high school, I didn't have money to go to college. I decided that I would work for several years to earn the money for college. I didn't have the slightest intention of being a newspaperman. I had vague notions of being a "writer", of a great novel, probably. Now did I seem to have aptitude for newspaper work. I have often said, from what I learned after hiring many people as an editor, that I would not have hired myself. Nor am I sure that I would have had the patience with me in my trying formative period that my first boss, F.R. Peters, had with me.

There were three newspapers in my home town of Evansville, Indiana. The morning *Courier*, the afternoon *Journal*, and the afternoon *Press*. The last had been started by the Scripps newspapers the year before. I chose the third, a little four-page sheet. Why? Because of the editorials. They had two qualities which were responsible for the rise of Scripps newspapers—human interest and readability—which we lost awhile and are now recovering. They had a third quality which we have never lost, but to which we need constant rededication—devotion to the interests of the 95 percent, and championing of the cause of the oppressed and unfortunate.

So I climbed the dark stairs of the little old building in the wholesale district where *The Press* was housed and asked for a job. There I first met the kindness of Scripps-Howard which I have met in many people in many places.

The first embodiment was in the smiling face of Ward C. Mayborn, business manager. What it meant to a lad just out of high school to be greeted as Ward Mayborn greeted me! He made me feel that nobody in the world was more important than I was. The fact that he is of distinguished appearance made his kindness all the more appreciated.

He explained that he was the business manager, that the editor, who hired the reporters, was away getting married, and would see me on his return. I hope I have been half as kind to the hundreds who have asked me for jobs as Ward Mayborn was to me.

I came back to see the editor. Here I met that Scripps-Howard kindness in another form. F. Romer Peters didn't have the easy affability, the unfailing charm that characterized Mayborn. He was abrupt, choleric, and did not communicate easily until he knew you well. But without his kindness I would never have got started, much less succeeded.

I brought him some high school news, and he was not repelled by the fact that the first item told of my class' graduation honors, including Edward J. Meeman in second place.

Years later I heard him say: "Modesty in a newspaperman is a crime." He may have said it lightly, but I took it seriously, and believe it is true.

The best newspapermen, I find, know when they have done good work and fully appreciate it and take pride in it. The only qualification is: You have to appreciate the other fellow's good work just as much. When you don't, your honest, healthy pride and self-confidence become the swelled head, and you are a poor team-mate. On *The Press-Scimitar* we give weekly cash prizes for outstanding work, and we nominate each other's work, and tell why. That makes friendship and good feeling and is good for our morale.

I got the job, at $4 a week, and I wasn't worth it.

For years I had read much out of the public library. One hot summer day I was reading a book by Ernst Haeckel, the German evolutionist. He said all was matter; mind and spirit were but the result of physical phenomena. He denied the immortality of the soul, the existence of God as I thought of God.

Haeckel wrote with a tone of authority, and I thought he

had it. Today I read in the Encyclopedia Britannica: "Haeckel occupies no serious position in the history of philosophy." How much unnecessary suffering there is because people believe what has already been discredited, because they do not know, or will not believe, the saving truth which has been firmly established as effective in human experience!

I thought there was no God—and I could not live without God. I became sick of soul, and then sick of body. My young legs were heavy as I went about my reporter's beat. It was a clear demonstration of the effect of thought on matter, but I was too miserable to take any comfort in that.

Then I remembered a woman I had met in covering church news. Mary Collson was a woman of New England descent. She had been a Unitarian minister in Iowa, and then gone with Jane Addams at Hull House. Overcome by the weight of the evil of the world as she saw it in the Chicago slums, she had become a Christian Science practitioner in order to cut off evil at its root by proving its unreality. She had been sent to Evansville by the Mother Church to meet a need they saw there. The building of a new church was announced. I went to see her to get a story about it.

"Then I suppose you will be having oyster suppers and bazaars to pay for it?" I asked.

"My dear boy, no!" she exclaimed. "We love our church and do not need any inducements to give to it."

This impressed me. It seemed a higher order of religion than I had known. I was also impressed with the beauty and peace of her office. On the wall there hung a copy of the well-known painting on the theme of Isaiah, "The lion and the lamb shall lie down together and a little child shall lead them." There were flowers on the table. Most of all I was impressed by Mary Collson, and the idealism that spoke from the clear blue eyes beneath the crown of braided hair.

In my despair I thought of her. "Maybe she can help me."

I went to see her. She told me of Christian Science. I resisted it. She got me to read *Science and Health*. I found it crude and disjointed. But I liked her.

One day she said just the right words:

"Immortality is just living. You are living your eternal life now. Live it a day at a time. As Emerson says: 'Trust the power that has brought you thus far in safety.' "

That did it. I was healed. I could work again in normal good spirits and energy. I no longer dragged my legs as if they were lead. I have never found those words in Emerson, though I have found the same thought implied.

Miss Collson was a theological liberal, a Unitarian. How fortunate I was to learn of Christian Science from such a one, because I saw that one could practice its great principles and get its benefits without believing the biblical myths which the Christian Science church accepts but which I had given up, such as the stories of Moses' rod becoming a serpent, the flaming horses and chariots round about Elijah, the young Hebrews who could be in a fiery furnace yet not get burned, the virgin birth of Jesus, or his physical resurrection and ascension. Mary Baker Eddy had been brought up in an orthodox household, and it was natural that she should put the new wine of Christian Science in the old bottles of fundamentalist conceptions, but it was equally natural for me who had become a theological liberal, to look for that in Christian Science which does not depend for its truth and practical effectiveness on these old orthodox conceptions, which I had found, and still find, mythical.

I regard Mary Baker Eddy as incomparably the greatest woman who ever lived and one of the greatest persons, man or woman, in all history. If she had done nothing but found the *Christian Science Monitor*, the best newspaper in the world, at the age of 87, she would still be one of the very great.

III

Joining the Socialist Party: "If You Can Stand It, We Can."—Covering the Labor Movement—Friendship With Eugene Debs—Sojourn in Cleveland—Back to the Minors

My father was a leader in the local cigarmaker's union. His fellow workers thought highly of him and his opinions. They would come to the house to see him on Sundays in order to get more of what they heard during the week. They lovingly brought him home when he went on his sprees—alas! not to be received in that home with equal love.

John Henry Meeman must have been a responsible, conservative labor leader or else his employer, the handsome and gentlemanly Philip Grill, would have used his drunkenness as an excuse to fire him, which he never did; he showed always that he regarded him as a valued employee. He even came to our house to ask him to come back to work.

Papa ran for the Legislature on the Populist ticket. The Populist party was an indigenous liberal, perhaps radical, political movement without admixture of European ideology. He was not elected. Some time later he became a Socialist. I remember as a boy of 10 or 12 being taken by my father to Germania Hall to hear Eugene V. Debs, candidate for president, who had led a national railroad strike. I have never heard a more effective orator. He spoke this first time I heard him in Germania Hall on how the two old parties were just alike, equally enemies of the workingmen, and how the workingmen should support their own party, the Socialist Party.

Later, as a young reporter, I was to introduce Debs myself
to a large mass meeting in my home town:

*(A speech introducing Eugene Debs at a Socialist Party meeting, delivered
at Evans Hall, Evansville, September 15, 1911)*

Once upon a time Eugene V. Debs was to address a meeting in an eastern town where there was a bitter prejudice against
him. The young man who was to introduce him thought he
ought to allay it. So he said:

"Debs is hated by some people because he has been in
strikes. That is not right. It is the law of nature to defend
yourself. Why even a dog will growl if you try to rob him of the
bone he is gnawing; a goat will butt if you get in his way, and you
all know what a jackass will do if you monkey with him.

"Ladies and gentlemen, this is Debs."

But if there was ever a Socialist in Evansville who thought it
necessary to apologize for introducing Debs, I am sure there is
none here today.

We are proud of this man who was imprisoned in
Woodstock, Ill., jail for the sake of the working class. We are
proud of his record of over 15 years of unceasing work in
unflinchingly, tirelessly bringing to the working class of
America the great good news that the settlement of the bread
and butter problem is ready for them to take to the ballot box.

We are proud of this great prophet of industrial righteousness. And how we love him. We love him for making us his
friends, but we also love him for the enemies he has made. Let
me present to you the man whom the Socialist Party of America
thrice has honored with the presidential nomination and who
has honored that workers' party by serving it well. Ladies and
gentlemen, let me present to you—Eugene V. Debs.

Like all true orators, Debs wasted no time on pre-
liminaries. He strode to the very front of the stage, his long,
lean, rangy body ready to reach out to the audience in direct
appeal.

In the most effective speech I ever heard him make, his
very first words were: "I want to talk to you about the McNamara boys!"

"The McNamara boys" were labor leaders, structural iron
workers, under arrest on charges of dynamiting the plant of the

Los Angeles *Times*, at that time the leading "open shop" newspaper in the country.

Debs roused his audience with an attack on the capitalists, who, he said, were conspiring to frame innocent labor leaders, champions of oppressed workers, and railroad them to prison.

A few months later, as a reporter for the *United Press* in Indianapolis, I was to be briefed by District Attorney Frank Dailey on the evidence he was laying before the federal grand jury—evidence which clearly showed the guilt of the McNamara "boys".

I am sure Gene Debs believed utterly in their innocence. His fellow workers could do no wrong. He loved and trusted everybody he knew. He even loved and trusted all the capitalists he knew personally—as they did him. It was the generic "capitalists" whom he had never met—"the capitalist class"—whom he denounced. The denunciation was impersonal—but with what power!

As a young boy I accepted my father's socialism. But in my later years in high school, I was too absorbed in the treasures of literature, history and languages to think much about the exploitation of the poor. Moreover, I was dazzled by the rich friends I made—the lovely girls who let me help them with their Latin lessons, the boys who showed respect for my precocity.

But after graduation I became a cub reporter, and I saw with my own eyes the men working 10 hours a day in factories, learned in reporting the labor union beat how difficult it was for them to have a labor union at a time when employers could root out and fire with impunity the "agitators" who dared to join.

One day I strode determinedly up to the desk of my boss, F. Romer Peters, the editor of the Evansville *Press*.

"I have joined the Socialist Party," I announced with defiant finality.

I think I expected to be fired right then, and martyred to the cause. At the least, I expected a choleric denunciation for my folly.

Mr. Peters—he was always "Mr." to me—did not look up

from the copy he was reading. He did not stop puffing his pipe. He said: "If you can stand it, we can."

What it means to say the right thing to a young person! That reply made a liberal of me for life.

If he had fired me, if he had even upbraided me. I might have become an extremist, a fanatic.

There are only a few people who really influence one, who change the direction of one's life. Mr. Peters was the greatest influence in mine. He became a second father to me. Although I should have respected my own father, I did not. I respected Mr. Peters. His treatment of me was like that of a father, not a boss. He alternately spoiled me with patience and personal interest, and dressed me down unmercifully. After he made me managing editor, he would come into the news room and bawl me out right before my staff. I would sit silent under the attack. Finally he would yell: "Why don't you say something?" Once he pitched a wastebasket across the room, turned on his heel and left.

He taught me everything he knew about newspaper work, and without that, I could never have succeeded. I admired him so much that I imitated his ways and some of his mannerisms. When I was on my own, I even found myself bawling out people who worked for me, as Peters had bawled out me—until I woke up and saw that a more discriminating practice of the example he had set me would do him more honor and me more good.

I learned from him that "a newspaper should have no client but the people;" should be "independent politically, financially, commercially;" that you should not allow an influential person to pressure you into keeping news out or suppressing an editorial which the public interest or your own integrity required.

I learned that everybody is busy with either work or pleasure, and therefore you take time to save the reader's time by reducing every story to the fewest possible words that would tell the story well.

I learned to be afraid of no one, not even of him—at least

never to be frightened out of doing what I thought I should.

I remember another occasion when as a cub reporter I learned volumes in a few words from him.

I came back from reporting a revival by a local minister of magnetic personality. I turned in my copy and said to the boss: "Don't you think he's wonderful?"

"If he's sincere," he said.

It had never occurred to me that a man who came in the name of God could be insincere. But I was to learn deeper wisdom about sincerity from Charles Clogston, a fellow reporter on the Terre Haute *Post*, who was backing Theodore Roosevelt while I was supporting the Socialists. Roosevelt was attacking my Socialist friends as immoral. And I didn't like it. I said: "T.R. is insincere." Clogston replied:

"Insincerity is the easiest of all charges to make and the hardest to prove."

About the same time my Socialist friend, Stephen Reynolds, said: "People always do what they think is right. If you didn't think it was right at the time, you wouldn't do it." But that is letting people off too easily.

I gave myself whole-heartedly to work for the Socialist party.

After my day's work was over at the paper, I would often go to the home of a tinner, Joseph Kaelin, for the evening. We gathered around his dining room table to work for the party. We would prepare notices and write letters. I would do the typing. We would arrange for speakers and literature distribution. Literature would be distributed Saturday night or early Sunday, to be found by the householder when he woke up.

(*Speech to Evansville Local of the Socialist Party, Evans Hall, September 15, 1911.*)

Ladies and gentlemen—comrades!

I appear before you in behalf of the local body which represents in Evansville a world-wide organization second in magnitude only to the Christian church, the teachings of which it is the practical application to politics and economics. This organization embraces men and women of 25 nationalities, and the principal races and colors. It represents 10 million voters and 25 million persons. It is the only international, worldwide political party on this planet, with an international convention elected by the party members in each nation. This organization extends wherever capitalism has brought the machinery or social means of production which the workers must use to get their living, but which they do not own and cannot use except at the terms dictated by the few who own that machinery. Though false statements to the contrary often have been made, yet we say quite positively that in all parts of the globe its principles and platforms are essentially the same. Everywhere, and always, it stands for the collective ownership and democratic management by the workers of all means of production, transportation, distribution and exchange. That is the Socialist party.

Local Evansville of that international party wishes me to ask you workers to unite with us in the great work of capturing the government, to get a guarantee that every grown-up and able-bodied person shall have the right to work and the opportunity to work—to do useful and beautiful work, to own his own job, and to receive the full social value of his work instead of a small part of it as he now does. I am sure that you know that we want you to vote with us but I am not so sure that you know how very, very much we want you who intend to vote with us to become members of the party organization. Reading Socialist literature and voting the ticket does not make one a Socialist. He is not a truly complete Socialist until he carries one of these cards, red like the blood of humanity of all nations for whose good cause it stands.

This card shows that its possessor has a vote to decide all important questions of the party's welfare and to direct and control the conduct of its officers through the initiative referendum and recall, not only in local but in state and national affairs as well. He controls even the proceedings of the international congress by electing the delegates to it. He not only subscribes to the platform and votes the ticket, but he does what is more important: he votes to make the platform and to nominate men for the ticket who are just what he thinks they should be, so that he can support them and ask his friends to support them fully and without apology. What right has a Socialist voter to knock on the party's way of doing business and to kick on the kind of platform and ticket it has put forward, if he has not accepted the party's invitation to come inside and help manage its affairs? The

Socialist Party will not be representative of the Socialists of the city unless they become members. Even if it is impossible for you to do active work we beg you to become a member so you can vote on the vital questions—by referendum, by mail if it is impossible for you to attend meetings.

There is another reason why the Socialist Party will not be your party completely unless you join it. Of course it takes money to carry on the business of the party, the propaganda work, the campaign work, and other things which make legitimate expenses. Where is the money to come from? Shall we accept contributions from the capitalist interests, as the Republican and Democratic parties have done? No, indeed! for then it would cease to be our party: it would belong to those capitalistic interests. A dog obeys the hand that feeds it: so does a political party. If the Socialist Party is to belong to the working class and represent the working-class perfectly, it must be financed by themselves entirely. The workers must pay for their own politics if it is really to be their own. That is why every Socialist is asked to become a member of the organization and pay the regular dues of 25 cents a month. No dues are required of members who are out of work and unable to pay.

I know that wages are so unjustly low in many cases that 25 cents a month seems a good deal to pay. But comrades, is it not a small price to pay for the only way to emancipate yourselves, your children and your class? Especially when you consider that many have laid down life itself in that cause.

So, if you are a Socialist, we ask you to come to one of our regular meetings which for the present are held every Wednesday night at Weber's Hall, Fourth Avenue and Franklin St., and take out a red card. If you are not ready to join, we shall be glad to have you come and see how the Socialist Party conducts business.

Now, comrades, Local Evansville is going to ask for a collection. We do not apologize for passing the hat. Without a collection this meeting would be impossible, as the quarters we have all paid at the door do not meet all the expenses. We can use the language of circus posters truthfully and say that the subscription cards to the *Appeal to Reason* are alone worth the price of admission, as 25 cents is the regular price for a 40-weeks subscription to that paper such as you are getting along with admission to the lecture.

Local Evansville is heavily in debt for this meeting, and only a generous offering on your part will make our books even.

The collectors will pass down the aisles presently, and for the sake of a Socialist organization in Evansville free from debt, I ask you to contribute freely. And now let me present to you George D. Brewer, manager of the *Appeal to Reason* lecture bureau. Comrade Brewer.

We would bring speakers for meetings, mostly on street corners. The speakers came from great distances, sometimes from abroad. These speakers were always people I was glad to meet. They were always idealists. One of these, a young red-haired woman of 17, Florence Wattles, became my lifelong friend. She became an editor of E. P. Dutton & Co., a Norman Thomas right-winger, one who knew the conspiring left-wingers for what they were and fought them.

(A letter to Florence Wattles, August 6, 1934)

Dear Florence:

I am writing this note separately because I thought you would want to show the letter about the book to someone, and this is personal.

For many weeks I have been reading the NEW LEADER which is brought to me faithfully each week by one of my subscribers, who thus hopes to enlighten the capitalist press—and he does!—and I have been much interested in the discussion of the Detroit declaration. Each week I have wondered what you think about it.

I believe this is what I think:

The Detroit declaration is a mistake. It is not a sign of new life, militancy, etc., as its authors vainly think. It is due to the socialists themselves being infected with the error of the times, which is to give value to violence and force and dictatorships, values which they do not really have.

The big mistake is their analysis of fascism. It is not so much a countermove of the capitalist class to prevent the triumph of socialism, as it is a result of the war psychology. That is, if a normal state of mind existed in a nation, the socialists, on attaining power through a majority vote, would not necessarily be met with a fascist movement.

What we see today is the aftermath of war, which disrupted normal conceptions of values.

What I hope to see is the deflation of this war aftermath. If, as may happen, fascism blows up first in Germany and then in Italy, and Russia continues to modify in the direction of liberalism, and economic nationalism gives way to a resumption of trade, then we may again enter a period of peaceful progress, and the young intellectuals who have declared liberalism—i.e., civilization—out of date, will be found singing very much out of tune.

In such a day the socialists will regret having made a Detroit declaration.

To me there is a fundamental inconsistency in opposing war and advocating "revolution." They are of the same nature, and both destructive of civilization.

But I would like to know what you think, if you have the time to answer.

Yours sincerely,
Ed

(Letter to Florence Wattles, July 4, 1935)

Dear Florence:

You do me a compliment to suggest that I write a book on Gene Debs, or try to. I don't think I have the ability to do the research required, and I am certain I have not the patience. Perhaps I would find the ability and develop the patience if I were out of a job.

Unless impelled by economic need, I think there is only one book I will ever write. I feel it now, deeply; I don't think I have the words yet; I may never have them. The theme would be Man's responsibility. Man so far is a failure; he can be a success. Not only is Man of free will; but the tragedy of human life is that he is so very free. Of course the Determinists are not wholly wrong; there is a vast equipment which is automatic. But the good or bad results—and they have been mostly bad—are not the result of the functioning of what is automatic. Human life is formed by Man's sense of values and his Will. It can be almost anything, very good or very bad; very interesting or very dull; very kind or very cruel. It is of supreme importance what Man believes and what he chooses to do. We are constantly at the standpoint of choice.

The Socialists are going to be bitterly disappointed when they discover that happiness will not result from their perfect economic system unless something else happens. For that perfect economic system will not remain perfect unless high moral values and spiritual energies have been brought into play to make it so. There was every reason to believe that the "free" economic system and political democracy conceived by the founders of this republic would result in a Utopia. There was nothing wrong with the conception: the same opportunity for all. Its failure has not been economic, but moral. If capitalism had been honestly and kindly practiced, the story would have been entirely different. And so it will be with collectivism. Unless it is saved by the introduction of moral values, the struggle for power will poison it as greed has poisoned capitalism.

Today's psychology is much occupied with study of the abnormal. But study will show that it is not the abnormal but the normal, who, finally, are to blame. The assassin of Sarejevo was a fanatic; but it was perfectly normal statesmen who lacked the moral grandeur to prevent that act from plunging Europe into war. So today, it was not the frantic Hitler who is really responsible for Germany's return to barbarism, but the perfectly balanced, coolly intellectual Allied statesmen, who were not morally big enough to do justice to democratic Germany.

Human nature, left to itself, falls to a low level of pettiness. It must stimulate itself with high ideals, constantly, and it must be careful how it chooses those ideals. For the false ideal—first "to make the world safe for democracy" and now "Italy must be an empire" and "We must win the class war"—these false ideals lead to disaster. And what are true ideals?—the ideals of peace, and love, and justice, and the improvement of the race.

Do these things sound ordinary, platitudinous? I fear they do. Yet truth is a platitude; if it were not recognized as obvious it would not be true. The world desperately needs to recognize and practice the obvious. You have heard of the man who knew a lot of things that were not so; the trouble today is that we do *not* know so many things that *are* so, have always been so, and always will be. We have hundreds of thousands of brilliant young intellectuals who relish a "class war"—not recognizing that by so naming it they have condemned it for what it is—war, and therefore evil. War was evil when religion was the subject of dispute; it was evil in 1917 when "liberty" and the "rights of small nations" were in dispute, and it is evil now, when "class" is in dispute.

What do you think of all this? Will I ever be able to write it in a fresh, challenging way, that I can attract attention to what is not new—for if it were new it would not be true, and hence wouldn't be worth saying.

No, my work does not bore me. But it does absorb all my energies. Perhaps some day I'll give it up—and write this book. If I could only write it!

I am about to leave for a Fourth of July picnic at an Arkansas plantation—delightful, pleasant people, but with whom I have little in common. That's what I miss—my "ain folk," people who care about these big things.

> My best,
>
> Edward J. Meeman

We were Christian Socialists. To us the class struggle was not something to be bitterly waged, but something to be ended by the peaceful triumph of socialism at the ballot box.

But there came into our easy-going happy benign group of humanitarians an immigrant from Kaiser Wilhelm's Germany. "Ve must have discipline!" he declared. He had been regimented, and he was determined to regiment us. He got control of the local. All of the spontaneity, all the love, all the fun, all the shining hope went out. There was only grim militancy. "We will go down to the newspapers and demand so much space for our propaganda and if they do not grant it we will boycott them," he announced.

Thus I learned that everybody who said they wanted socialism did not have the same idea as those of us who wanted lovingly to win a majority to a system in which everybody would have everything and everybody would be happy. They were more sinister than the capitalists who allowed a 10-hour day in the furniture factories of Evansville.

It was early experiences like these that made me immune to the appeal of Communism, which deceived so many idealists like myself during the Depression and later. How grateful I am that I learned the nature of the Left Wing, the illiberal liberals, so early in life!

I knew whose side I would be on. I resigned from the local. I had found that I couldn't "stand it," as that gruff boss with the soft heart no doubt had known all the time that I couldn't.

I was through with proletarianism but I was not through with socialism. Taking an interest in my career which I was not yet ready to take myself, my boss got me a job with the national feature and editorial organization of which our paper was a member, the Newspaper Enterprise Association, with headquarters in Cleveland, Ohio. He thought I needed a broader field and a varied experience.

I joined the Socialist Party local in Cleveland. There were picnics and dances. There were hot debates at the meetings. Here again I found those who would regiment us. I found myself in opposition to the left wing headed by C.E. Ruthenberg. He later went to prison for opposing World War I and was known as a Communist. I was startled the other day to see in NBC's pictures taken inside the Kremlin that there is a tablet on the walls in honor of Ruthenberg, just as there is one of John Reed.

I prepared the Labor Day service for the Newspaper Enterprise Association. I could present a picture of labor, of moderate socialism, of humanitarian legislation advancing all over the world. It was a happy picture of progress, which then stretched forth endlessly. It was 1910.

(From NEA Labor Day Round-Up, August 27, 1910)

How do the laboring people of the world stand on this Labor day, at the end of the first decade of the twentieth century?

The (name paper) has asked its correspondents everywhere, and they report that labor's progress the world over during the first decade of the century was so great that it is not too much to believe that it will have wiped out poverty when the century's last decade is passed.

The labor movement is the biggest movement today, and it is the only universal secular movement. In some form it appears in every country. It is a movement to raise wages, shorten hours, and improve conditions in the trade where the union men work today. In its political aspects it aims at clean and efficient government. It is the expression in deeds of the creed common to ALL religions that men should work for each other's good.

It is a movement primarily of the workers themselves, but an increasing number of philanthropic aristocrats step down from the backs of labor to work WITH instead of FOR labor, for they know they can do the most good that way.

Reports from foreign countries, given below, show that while the condition of the workingmen is better in America than anywhere else, yet the rate of labor's progress is faster in other countries.

Inventions have, of course, raised the standard of living of the modern workingman far above that of the kings in the Middle Ages. The condition of all classes in America is above that of all classes in other countries, yet the working people of America have been less determined to catch up with the capitalists in taking part in the benefits of the improved conditions.

An intense optimism and a determination that the resources of the world shall be so systematically used that "everybody shall have everything" pervades the labor movement today.

There are four ways to the goal of the labor movement. First, the trades unions, wherein the workingmen unite in dealing with their employer to secure better conditions. Second, the workingmen's parties, by which they secure representation in the government, to get favorable laws and cause the government to engage in industry as an employer of workingmen. Third the co-operatives, in which the workers voluntarily associate themselves, to produce together (employing themselves and owning their own jobs), and to sell and buy together, eliminating waste in profit. Fourth, measures taken by the government and employers voluntarily to improve the workers' condition.

BRITONS IN POLITICS

Forced into politics against their will 10 years ago, the labor unions of Great Britain have played the game with a zeal undreamed of by their colleagues in the United States. Today no measure is sure of easy passage through the House of Commons unless the compact phalanx of 40 Labor members is for it.

The employees of the Taff Vale railway, in Wales, had struck. The company sued the railway mens' union for damages caused by the strike and seized the union's funds. The courts allowed the railway to keep the union's funds.

For six years thereafter no union dared to strike. The Taff Vale judgment made it lawful for any employer to attach the war chest of the employees who dared to strike against any conditions he was pleased to impose.

During these six years the labor leaders studied politics and organized the labor party to nullify the Taff Vale judgment. In 1896 organized labor sent 30 members to parliament to the unutterable disgust of the fine old Tory gentlemen, who wondered what the country was coming to when workingmen could become the M.P.'s.

Result: The Taff Vale judgment is no longer operative.

English lawmakers are not paid. Before organized labor entered politics, no Englishman ever dreamed of trying for Parliament except as a climax to a prosperous career.

None of the Labor candidates is even well-to-do. To meet this expense of running and holding office the rank and file of the unions were assessed a shilling a year for campaign purposes.

English workingmen know now that the unjust Taff Vale judgment was the luckiest thing that ever happened to them since it awakened them to the necessity of entering politics.

From that year the labor movement began to grow as never before. . . .

Successful politics; then lawmaking.

The party secured an improved "workmen's compensation act." The old act was full of anomalies. One instance: A workman injured while putting the first or second coat of paint on a building could recover compensation, but not if injured while putting on the third or fourth coat. The first and second coats were "construction," while the third and fourth were "decoration."

In the first year after it became law, in seven industries alone, 328,931 persons received $10,403,360 in compensation.

The miners' eight-hour law was first introduced over 20 years ago, but not until labor sat as an independent force in the House of Commons was it passed.

The Liberal Party passed the old-age pension bill, but not

until the labor unions made it an issue and forced it upon the government.

The Labor Party is now working for effective factory and mining inspection. . . .

Women are raggedly organized in England with the exception of the textile workers in the north. Theirs is a work that does not suffer from male competition; the working women are of an exceptionally fine class, and the latest statistics show that 90 per cent of them are unionized in the great mill centers. . . .

Though opposing war, the labor movement is really the most patriotic in England. It is working for healthful conditions to rebuild a race which is small and narrow-chested because of the child labor and woman labor of its parents, starved by poverty and deprived by unemployment.

IN GERMANY

Third in numbers, the trades unions of Germany are fast becoming the most powerful in the world. There are now 1,800,000 in trades unions, and it is freely predicted that the Social-Democratic party, which is supported by nearly all of the trades unions, will control the empire before the twentieth century is half gone.

Prosperous co-operative movements, engaged in everything from soapmaking to banking, reduce the cost of living for the working people engaged in them. There are 14,272 credit societies, 1883 stores, 3062 agricultural, 199 other productive societies, and 2500 for other purposes. . . .

Germany has more strikes than any other nation of Europe.

IN FRANCE

The government of France is so anxious to please the trades unions that Paris and 111 other cities have established *bourses de travail*, where they can meet to organize and plan strikes! Over fifty-two cities, too, have opened employment agencies, but they are inferior to the German. The labor unions have a franking privilege in communicating with the government.

The government has also encouraged co-operation by appropriations. There are over 1200 co-operatives of various kinds, including many bakeries.

There are over 800,000 unionists in France, and they are getting stronger all the time.

IN AUSTRIA

Born in oppression, the labor movement of Austria-Hungary has almost attained liberty, and is one of the most rapidly growing movements in the world. The same men who formerly went to jail for advocating the cause of labor are now sent to the lawmaking body by the organized workers.

First labor organized politically, and then industrial unions were launched by the political leaders. They have grown rapidly. The government harasses the union. The workers get around the law which prohibits the union from paying strike benefits, by subscribing for a labor newspaper which pays benefits when its subscribers "quit at the same time."

Laws discriminate in favor of aristocracy. Workingmen must serve in the armies for three years; college graduates but one. Many workingmen have not the right of suffrage; in Hungary, not one man in twenty has a vote. . . .

There are nearly 700,000 organized men in Austria-Hungary.

IN ITALY

In Europe the trades unions are organized and often led by "intellectuals," well-educated men, who though not workingmen themselves, feel the sting of aristocratic oppression which is so sharp there, and take up the cause of labor. In contrast to America, "sympathizers" who belong to no union are admitted freely to the central city bodies.

In Italy this is especialy true. In agricultural southern Italy, whence come most of the emigrants to America, labor is poorly organized, but in industrial northern Italy the unions are rapidly gaining power; industrial, political and co-operative organizations are joined into one movement. In Milan, particularly, where the labor representatives have a majority in the government, the working people own co-operative stores, printing offices, newspaper, tenement buildings, hotel and central office buildings. . . .

The significant thing about the movement is its domination of the municipalities.

AUSTRALIA

Labor has its own way in Australia. For the first time in the history of that continent has one party a majority over all possible combinations that can be formed against it, and that party is the Labor Party.

With a population of but 4,000,000 in a country of vast and hardly scratched resources, Australia has not many economic problems. But one thing the Labor government finds it necessary to do at once is to lay a heavy tax on the great estates which absentee landlords hold out of use, to break them up into small farms for the people to work.

BELGIAN WORKERS

Belgium is the home of the truest co-operation in the world. Many stores and industries are owned and run by the workers. As the stores deal only with members, no one makes any profit off another. There are 1,200 co-operatives, with a membership of nearly 200,000.

The members of the Vooruit, in Ghent, not only supply themselves with bread and shoes through its many stores, but they also get medical services, art, music, drama, athletics, books, education, and trips abroad for child pupils through the organization. . . .

The organization in the industrial field is not so flourishing as that in the co-operative and political movements. Wages are very low, but rising.

There are about 100,000 in the unions.

LABOR'S PARADISE

New Zealand is the one country where the working people get things without fighting for them. The government runs all public utilities, including banks and coal mines, compels arbitration of labor disputes, guarantees titles, buys all patents, acts as trustee for estates, gives free railroad passes to men seeking work, gives unemployed work in state forests until they find a better job, requires seats for girls in stores, and makes loans to home builders.

Groups of workmen may organize, elect a foreman, and the state lets public work to them. Thus the contractor is eliminated. The Saturday half-holiday is universal in factories.

LABOR IN THE ALPS

From time immemorial Switzerland has been a good place for workaday folks. Now the unions have obtained such recognition that a "workman secretary," whose salary is paid by the federal government, is elected by the labor unions. The labor question has never been an acute one in Switzerland, owing to the purely democratic spirit that pervades all ranks of society there.

Factory employees are allowed to work on their little Alpine farms during the summer season. An average of one member in each family is a member of a co-operative. The cheese industry is controlled by co-operatives. Co-operation has made an 8-cent dinner of soup, meat and vegetables possible in Basel.

Basel is the headquarters of the International Association to Promote Labor Legislation, which is trying to get uniform labor laws in all countries, so that one country will not have a commercial advantage over another because of more lax laws. Right now it is devoting itself principally to laws regulating woman and child labor.

IN OTHER LANDS

Denmark takes the lead in labor activity in Scandinavian countries. It has possibly the most complete labor organization in the world. The trades unions have increased wages and shortened hours in nearly all industries. They have also organized the rural workers. They have secured old-age pensions and improved factory conditions for the workers, and are working to replace the slums with model homes. . . . There are over a thousand co-operative stores.

The great general strike in Sweden last year not only strengthened the labor movement there, but drew the Scandinavian movements and those of other countries closer together. There are 150,000 trades unionists in Sweden. The growing co-operative movement is building "houses of the people" in the cities which become centers of labor activity. The workers are fighting for universal suffrage.

In Norway the industrial and political labor movements are one. Labor laws are fair. There is workmen's compensating and state insurance. Women may not work in mines or at machines. Christiania lends workmen money to build homes of their own.

In Finland the labor movement gained almost half of the representation in the Diet, and conducts a prosperous co-operative movement.

In Holland the unions are divided by religion, and somewhat by anarchy. A state commission composed of both capitalists and laborers is investigating the unemployment problem. . . .

In countries where the common people are not represented in the government, the labor movement is engaged
almost entirely in revolutionary struggles to get these political
rights, which are necessary before they can act safely in the
industrial field. Such countries are Russia, Spain, Portugal,
Turkey and the Balkan countries, Persia, Egypt, India, China,
Japan, Mexico and other Spanish-American countries. In these
countries labor is in a condition of slavery, because the tyrannical governments crush any attempt of the working people to
better their conditions by the strike . . .

I was not ready for the majors, and was sent back to the
minors, and my old boss took me back. I was fired, but my
vanity didn't let me recognize that at the time; I thought I had
quit. My boss was now publisher of two papers, the one in
Evansville and one in Terre Haute, *The Post*. He gave me a job
in Terre Haute.

There I again met socialism. I met it mostly in the men of
the United Mineworkers, whose district office I covered. I
thought the Mineworkers ought to be more militant, that they
were not as much interested in their cause as I was, but now I
realize they knew what they were doing.

One of the Socialist speakers we had brought to Evansville
was Stephen Marion Reynolds, a lawyer. One night coming out
of a movie, I met him. With him was his red-haired wife,
Jessica.

"Come and have a steak with us," she said.

I became part of a circle of older people which included
Gene Debs, though most of them were not Socialists. I found
that everybody in Debs' home town loved him, including the
conservative business and professional men, not only because
of his wife, who was a member of the wealthy Baur soda
fountain family of Chicago, but for himself. I was taken to see
Debs. He remembered me from the time I had introduced him
at Evansville, greeted me warmly. He saw me as one of the
younger men he hoped would carry on the movement when he
had passed out of the picture, and told me so.

He went to Atlanta Federal Prison for opposing World War I. As a friend of his I was asked by the Newspaper Enterprise Association to go there to interview him. Outwardly, it was a cheerful meeting. I was sad inside, as I saw him walk to greet me in his prison suit. We sat and talked.

(Page 1 Story, Evansville Press, March 25, 1920)

FEDERAL PENITENTIARY, ATLANTA, March 25—

"I do not have to make a campaign—the United States Supreme Court and Attorney General Palmer are making it for me," said Eugene V. Debs.

The Socialist leader, clad in prison garb of gray jacket and blue coat, and yet a candidate for the presidency of the United States, gazed through iron bars as he talked.

Debs, color-bearer of American Socialists in four other campaigns. looks a little older now than on the day of his conviction for his opposition to war measures.

The lines have deepened about his mouth and eyes. He looked a long time at the new green of the landscape beyond the spiked walls.

"I am not in prison," he said. "My spirit soars beyond those brown walls. My campaign speeches, though they be inaudible, are heard across the land. No, I have not been suppressed."

He talked first of politics. "The U.S. Supreme Court has declared that U.S. Steel Corporation was not a trust and annulled the anti-trust law.

"It declared there was no tax on stock dividends and the government lost a billion dollars that would have paid its soldiers' bonuses.

"A. Mitchell Palmer's compromise let the packers escape antitrust prosecution.

"What better campaigning could I have than this?"

Debs was a hospital clerk here first.

"I liked it," he said. "The inmates came to me with their troubles. Sometimes I could help them. Then they found that I would write letters for them and this one part of my work became so heavy that the prison authorities feared for my health."

The authorities wanted Debs to spend more time in the open air stockade and less time indoors. Finally they changed his occupation and a New York lawyer took over the letter writing.

"He and I helped a fellow the other day," said Debs and the wistful eyes turned again to the green fields outside. "He heard by the same mail that his wife was a mother and that he would be arrested when he left the prison in a few days on a second charge. We fixed it up and now he's free and with her."

There have been rewards, Debs says, for what he has done in prison and he is proud of them.

"A man with a useless left arm told me he would give his right hand, too, if I were free," Debs said. "A Negro found a four-leaf clover in the yard. 'You take it,' he said, 'so you'll be free instead of me.' I liked that."

But it was of the "revolution" that Debs wanted to talk.

"I don't think I'll be elected president," he smiled.

"There may never be a Socialist president, yet each concession of the reactionaries to the revolutionists makes them eager for greater concession and in this fashion the freedom of the worker will come."

Talk turned to Russia.

"If it was right for Russia to suspend free speech and free press was it not also right for the United States to suspend free speech in your case during the war?" Debs was asked.

"No," replied Debs. "The Russian revolution was a forward step. American participation in the war was a reactionary step. In suppressing me, because I was a revolutionist, a backward step was taken."

Debs speaks of Russia as "that great experiment in democracy;" he defends Lenin and as president would recognize his government.

The League of Nations hardly interests him.

"I believe in a league of peoples," he averred. "This can never be under a capitalistic system. Governments profess themselves in favor of a league against war and build their navies larger and increase their soldiery."

When he speaks of his life in the prison the convict-candidate's voice is soft.

"There is no criminal type," he said. "There are thugs, thieves and degenerates here—made so by circumstance. There are well-developed, intelligent men here, gone wrong for love of money. None of them should be in prison. Some should be in hospitals, others in asylums. They are the men the world

calls dangerous, yet not one of them has spoken unkindly to me
and I would not fear them anywhere.

"If the world only knew that love overcomes hate always
and that love conquers the beast in man!"

His attorneys tell Debs that he can be free on a writ of
habeas corpus since, they say, his transfer from Moundsville to
this prison was not according to law.

But Debs says:

"No pardon for me but an unconditional one. I am learning
things here."

Debs has asked his wife not to come to see him, for he
believes that such a visit, only to have the door close again
between them, would make the separation harder for both to
bear.

He was the same old Gene Debs. He told me what "fine
boys" his fellow prisoners were. Still the same lovable, gullible
Gene, unable to see any evil in anyone he knew personally,
whether it was a capitalist or a convict. It was only an impersonal "capitalist class" that he could denounce. Debs was what
Communists were later to call an "innocent." If he ever seemed
to condone the ruthlessness of left-wingers it was because he
could not believe they were doing what they were doing.

It was an even sadder meeting when I ran into Mrs. Debs
in the Terre Haute railroad station on her way to visit in prison
the man she loved, dressed in black which made more tragic
her beautiful pink complexioned face beneath its white hair.
How could this have happened to a man whom she knew to be
so good?

What do I think of socialism now?

I believe in both private enterprise and government enterprise. I think they should cooperate and sometimes com-
pete in peaceful coexistence. We should have a mixed economy
consisting of private enterprise, government enterprise, co-
operatives, partnerships, and self-employment.

I said government enterprise—not government operation
by a bureaucracy. I supported the Tennessee Valley Authority
even before it was created and fought in its defense. TVA has
succeeded because its executives and employees are selected,

neither by corrupting politics nor a deadening civil service, but by a merit system.

I do not believe in state socialism, but I do believe in private socialism—that is, in a profit-sharing capitalism.

The important question is not what economic form we have, but what are the ethical and business standards which govern it.

IV

Founding the Knoxville News: Formula for Newspaper Success—Private Remorse; Back to Christian Science—The High Life in Miami Beach

There came an expansion period of the Scripps-Howard newspapers. My boss, Romer Peters, took me with him to the annual Scripps-Howard conference of editors in Washington. It was the 1921 meeting.

We had not been in session long until he said to me: "Bob Scripps wants to see you. He wants you to start a newspaper in Nashville."

"Oh, I've always wanted to go to Nashville," I said in glee.

The truth was that I wanted to get out from under Peters' thumb. I loved and respected him, but I wanted to see what I could do on my own, practicing what he had taught me. I didn't know how much I wanted to get away until the opportunity came. When I saw Bob Scripps, it turned out that I was to go to Knoxville, Tenn., which I had heard of vaguely, if at all. It made no difference, any city that was not my home town would do.

The adventure of starting a newspaper, rare in this century, is one of the finest a young man can have—I was 32 years old. The prospect delighted and engrossed me. I had no personal or spiritual problems at the time. In high school, whatever inferiority complex I had was not troublesome, because I was an exceptional student and much repected by teachers and fellow students. Nobody cared that I was not very good in basketball and an indifferent swimmer, so I didn't care either. But I was not a very good reporter, and I had no feeling of success. Then, about 1916, Peters had said: "Bob Gore is going to Terre Haute. I want you to take the desk." Bob was the managing editor. Peters was publisher of both Scripps-Howard papers. "I can't do that!" I exclaimed. "I think you can," he said quietly. And so I took the desk. I succeeded, though by the hardest. I had to work 12 hours a day to do all that had to be done and to do it as well as I wanted it done. Peters had made a powerful, challenging newspaper, but I put better writing, more thorough coverage, a richer content into it.

(Editorial from the Evansville Press, March, 1919.)

THOSE WHO OPPOSE LEAGUE OF NATIONS RESEMBLE LAFOLLETTES AND LAMONTES

Those who in March, 1919, are opposing the proposition that the United States enter the League of Nations are like the Senator LaFollettes in Congress and the Frank LaMontes in Evansville, who in March, 1917, were trying to keep the United States from entering the war against Germany.

In 1917, those who opposed our entering the war said that we should not depart from the policy of isolation which they said Washington had laid down. They said that the affairs of Europe were not our affairs. They said we should confine ourselves to defending the shores of America, and let the Allies shift for themselves. They said that if we once "interfered" in European affairs, there would be nothing left of our Monroe Doctrine forbidding European nations to conquer American territory. . . . But we brushed all these objections aside. We saw that it was not a question whether we "wanted" to go to Europe to whip Germany or not. We saw that if we didn't go to Europe to help the Allies lick Prussian militarism over there, the conquering Germans would come over here and we would have the whole job to do alone. We saw that if we didn't intervene in Europe, the Kaiser would intervene in America. . . . We went into the war and we came out of it a better organized, more democratic, stronger, cleaner, broader, kinder nation. None of the fears of the pacifists as to what war-making would do to us was realized. Who now doubts that we did the ONE RIGHT THING?

Today there is a great debate on as to whether we should enter the League of Nations. It is objected that we would be involved in foreign dissensions, that our freedom of action would be restricted, that great burdens of keeping peace in distant parts of the world would be laid upon us. We are told that it would be better if we kept our "hands off."

But, as in the matter of making war on Germany, we have no choice. We cannot keep out of "foreign dissensions," for it was the little spark at Sarajevo which started the conflagration that finally attacked our ships on the seas, our factories in our own country and the safety of our own border. The modern world is so joined together that there is no land so distant but it may menace our safety. We cannot "go it alone."

We have either got to be ready to join with some other nations in a fighting alliance after war has broken out or we can enter into a covenant now with all the strong nations of the world TO ESTABLISH THE INTERNATIONAL JUSTICE WHICH WILL PREVENT WARS. And for us, the strongest, richest nation in the world, TO REFUSE NOW TO ENTER SUCH A LEAGUE, when the whole world is looking for our help and unselfish leadership, WOULD BE AS GREAT A STAIN ON OUR NATIONAL HONOR AS WOULD HAVE BEEN OUR REFUSAL TO DO OUR PART IN THE WAR AGAINST GERMANY. It would be, as former President Taft said at Evansville, to brand us as the "great slacker nation."

We believe that the question whether or not the United States shall enter a league of nations is as CLEAR A QUESTION BETWEEN RIGHT AND WRONG as was that of whether or not we should go to war with Germany. And WE HAVE NO DOUBT AS TO HOW THE PEOPLE OF AMERICA WILL ANSWER IT.

After a year, Max Dejong, who owned the quality ladies store of the town said: "Now you've got a newspaper," and started advertising with us. But working under Peters could never be easy, and I wasn't sure of myself.

I entered Knoxville wearing an authentic badge of success, Scripps-Howard's trust in me, to start a new newspaper for them. I had something else which gave me serene confidence, which I will explain in a moment, and I felt no need of religious consolation—Walt Whitman and a vague application of Christian Science sufficed.

Not because it offered religious consolation but because it was an outpost of free thought, and was interesting, I attended what was hopefully called "First" Unitarian Church. I remember with gratitude kindly, wise, Dr. A. R. Scott, the pastor, and this remark of his which has proved unforgettable:

"Life is too big to be reduced to a formula."

True, and the statement has kept me from ever accepting one religion alone to the exclusion of others, even Unitarian*ism*, as I don't like to hear it called.

Life cannot be reduced to any *one* formula, but formulas can be true and, in living, highly useful.

I would never have succeeded in Knoxville without the formula I brought with me. Without it, the knowledge that Scripps-Howard had enough confidence in me to put the Knoxville venture in my hands wouldn't have sufficed. I thought that the Scripps-Howard formula for newspaper publication, as exemplified and taught to me by Romer Peters, would win quick success in any city as it had in Evansville. It was simple:

"The publisher will have no economic interest except in newspapers, no affiliation or tie-ups, and hence be independent financially, commercially, politically. The editor will have complete control of what goes in the paper, including editing of advertisements. The editor will have precedence over the business manager, whose prerogatives, however, he respects. The editor will print all the news, even though it might embarrass advertisers and the politically powerful or members of the paper's own staff, even the editor himself."

(Letter to a disgruntled former subscriber to the Memphis Press-Scimitar,
December 8, 1932.)

Dear Mr. ————:

It is with regret that I learn that you have ceased to become a subscriber to *The Press-Scimitar* after having been a reader of our paper for seven years. It seems to me you would not have given this newspaper your attention every day for so long a period unless you had confidence in its integrity of purpose and in its willingness to tell the truth and voice its honest opinions regardless of the effect on the selfish interest of the newspaper. Therefore, I ask you, Mr. _____, would *The Press-Scimitar* be worthy to come into your home if I should say, "Come back and be a subscriber again and rest assured that we will go light on the railroad question from now on and you will never see anything in *The Press Scimitar* that you will disagree with or that will offend you." What would you think of such a newspaper or such an editor?

But this I can assure you: If some day you see fit to become a subscriber of The *Press-Scimitar* again, you will find in it a newspaper unfettered by any special interest (even its own). It will use its best thought and efforts to find out what is best for the public as a whole. Before printing an editorial we shall not ask ourselves, "If we print this will we lose any advertising, will we lose any subscribers?" We shall only ask, "Is this what ought to be said in the public interest?" Not that we shall always be right. We shall make mistakes, serious ones, perhaps. But they will be honest mistakes.

If we think the railroad interests deserve criticism we shall criticize them. If we think they need praise or defense we will praise or defend them. And the same with truck interests or waterway interests. But our policy will never be based on the desire to make a hit with any certain group or fear of offending any certain group. Had our policy been based on such consideration, you would not have read in our paper the criticism of the bus lobby several years ago when they ran their franchise bill through the legislature by corrupt means any more than you would have read more recently our criticism of certain railroad policies.

Again expressing our regret that you are no longer with us and hope that you may some day return,

Yours sincerely,
Edward J. Meeman

"The staff will write everything readably and as briefly as possible—as I put it, take time to save the reader's time; everybody is busy, either at work or pleasure. As Robert F. Paine, the first editor of the first Scripps newspaper, which had been founded by E.W. Scripps himself, reminded other editors to put human interest first: 'Some of our readers have brains, some have pocketbooks, but they all have hearts.' Take care of the 95 per cent of the people—the five per cent are powerful enough to take care of themselves. (It is no longer true that the five per cent can take care of themselves; they too now need a crusading newspaper to defend them from injustice.) Let the people be your only client. Use many pictures—a picture is worth a thousand words. Get the background, the lowdown, as well as the bare facts."

This formula has come to be applied by many newspapers, but then it was almost exclusive with Scripps-Howard.

Today I would add to the formula Roy Howard's statement: "Don't color the news, but give the news its own color." News is not gray, or black and white, it is rich with varied colors, and so the reporter should portray it. If he does not, he is not giving a true picture.

So it was not self-confidence so much as confidence, in a formula, or in principles, which enabled me to succeed in Knoxville. But editorial success would have not been enough, if the paper had not been undergirded with business success. The business manager, Myron G. Chambers, a former banker of Oklahoma City, who came to join the paper a year after it was launched, also had principles, which went far to explain his success.

Soon after he came, I told him I was about to buy a suit of clothes, and would he suggest which of our advertisers I should patronize. He answered:

"Every merchant in this city is either an advertiser in *The Knoxville News*, or a potential advertiser. You get your suit where you can make the best buy, and we will also sell our advertising on its merit."

He would never sell an advertisement if he did not think it would be worth to that particular advertiser, considering his particular needs, what it would cost. Often he would say of a proposal, "It's sound," or "It's not sound."

These lessons in ethics which I got from the business manager I never forgot. I owe much to Myron Chambers.

The precedence of the editor over the business manager is required by the relative nature of their responsibilities, but editors should never take a holier-than-thou attitude toward business managers.

As I waited for Robert P. Scripps in his sitting room in Washington's Wardman Park Hotel, on that day in 1921, I saw a copy of George Bernard Shaw's *Back to Methuselah* lying on the table. I thought even more of Scripps-Howard to find that the controlling stockholder or his wife was a reader of Shaw, who had been a moral influence in my life.

I had become managing editor at $25 a week. When the boss gave me a substantial raise I remarked to him: "I am not working for money." Then I read *Major Barbara* and its preface. I learned that money gives power and the effectiveness and freedom that go with power. From that time I accepted with gratitude all the money that came to me as the result of useful endeavor, and enjoyed doing good with it.

Bob Scripps got to the point quickly. "We will let you paddle your own canoe," he said. Then he said: "If you aren't able to succeed, we can't help you; if you are able, you won't need our help." So I was to be entrusted with capital that would either make money for them, or they would write it off with good grace as a venture that had failed. Exciting and thrilling—on my own!

"But I have just one piece of advice," he went on. "Some Northern-born men who go South think they can solve the Negro problem. They can't. You can't. The best you can do is not to do anything against the Negroes."

What a wise caution this was! It saved me from the possibility that I would be carried away by the reckless zeal of a crusader, and end in futility.

But I found that Knoxville, situated in hill country, was hardly more Southern than Evansville, my home town; in some respects less so. East Tennessee tried to stay with the Union in

the Civil War. There was a large infusion of Southerners in
Evansville; two of the best friends of my young manhood were
from aristocratic Kentucky families, Alex Hardigg and Richard
Waller.

The advice, though, proved its value when later I moved
to Memphis, where it tempered my zeal somewhat, though the
time soon came when I had been South long enough to know
what I was doing and could move from negative to positive and
begin to do something *for* the Negroes, as some of my
Southern-born friends themselves had begun to do.

I had a three-room apartment in Knoxville. I invited
David Buchanan, who had come from a small upper East
Tennessee town to be a reporter on the paper, to share it with
me. He was stricken with appendicitis and died before he got
the medical attention that would have saved him.

I was sickened with remorse. I thought if I had taken more
interest in him, had cared what he did in his leisure hours, had
been more intimate with him, I would have known he was ill
and would have saved him. But I had let him go his way and I
went mine.

Later I saw that I had suffered from a morbid conscience,
that there was no reason why I should have blamed myself. He
was a mature man, and there was no reason why I should have
intruded into his life.

But there was no doubt that David's death had plunged
me into a deep depression which caused me to suffer and made
me ill. And, as I had done when the first crisis in my life, the
loss of religious faith, had similarly plunged me into depression and illness, I turned to Christian Science for succor.

I applied to Mrs. J. Cuyler Kimball, who had been Mary
Allison, daughter of a Southern judge, and was now married to
a Knoxville lumberman. She was a class-taught student of
Christian Science and, as such, a practitioner, though her
name was never in the Journal. As a young married woman she
had been healed in Christian Science of what two of the best
physicians in town had diagnosed as cancer. After the diagnosis
the doctors asked her to rest a month to build up her strength

for an operation. In this period she studied Christian Science and became convinced of its truth. When after a month had elapsed the doctors re-examined her they were astounded to find no symptoms. After his healing she went into the vastnesses of the Great Smoky Mountains, then a remote wilderness, with a woman friend, Mrs. Iverson Graves, also a Christian Scientist, and there, in meditation, had a deep spiritual experience which continued to bear fruit all her life. Only recently she told me of a new experience, in which the sense of the continuity of life after death, the sense that she was now living an eternal life, came to her strongly, and doubt was impossible.

It did not take long for me to snap out of any attack of morbid conscience and deep depression. But the experience began a friendship with Mrs. Kimball which was one of the finest of my life. Walt Whitman said of himself, "I am the cheer-bringing god." Mary Kimball is the cheer-bringing goddess. She is the most joyous person I have ever known. She makes joyous not only the larger, but the smaller things in life. Gay and bright are words that must also be used. Even when she is troubled, and she is, sometimes, the trouble never brings or implies any doubt that life itself is wholly good, if only people would wake up and think and act right. In Knoxville society—and it was in society that I met her—there was no one more popular or sought after. Her gaiety and charm were eagerly sought by the conventional who never thought of accepting her religion, which was its source. She was not a narrow religionist. Much of her inspiration she had got from Emerson.

I went to the Christian Science Church frequently with Mrs. Kimball and it was a happy experience.

My mother died of cancer in 1928. I asked an Episcopal minister to give the funeral service, and that church's service is indeed simple and beautiful.

(Undated letter, probably 1921, to Mary Elisabeth Schulte Meeman.)

Dearest Mother—

Do you know I have learned at last to really appreciate your

dear, sweet self. I am homesick for you already—and for Gertrude, too—and you are always affectionately in my thoughts—
Your loving,
Ed

After the funeral he called on me and asked me to join the Episcopal church.

"But I don't believe all you believe," I said.

"All we ask is a good intention."

I admired the inclusiveness which led him to say this, though I did not accept the generous invitation. I am sure there are many Episcopalians who are quite meticulous in accepting the theology of their church and expecting other members to do so. I am sure there are others who find it a happy home without believing, or taking seriously, the theology. I have always enjoyed attending the Episcopal church under any circumstances. If it were nothing more than an expression of the tolerance and grace of the Anglo-Saxon temperament, it would justify itself. But it is much more.

I shall tell later how I met orthodox Episcopalians, culminating in the great Sam Shoemaker, and got much of my present religion from them, though remaining a religious liberal theologically.

The ethical-religious experience of working for a true idea and system which brings out the best in human nature is one of the best things in life. I had such an experience in supporting and fighting for council-manager government as administered by Louis Brownlow. Other such true ideas are Profit-sharing, Competition of diverse economic systems, Federation of the free and democratic nations.

Most of my life in Knoxville was engrossed with accomplishment in newspaper work, and through that, projects for what I thought was the common good.

After my mother's death in 1928, I went to Florida in the winter of 1928-1929. I went to the then best hotel in Miami Beach, the Pancoast, and settled down for enjoyment, at a cost of what then was many dollars per day. I ate magnificent table d' hote meals as I looked out over the blue Gulf Stream.

I got in with a crowd of Chicago millionaires, and went dancing in night clubs with them. They alluded to champagne simply as "wine"—they drank no other kind. However, there was no excess.

There was a man whom I then thought of as an "old" bachelor, one of the crowd.

"What's a young man like you doing down here at this time of year—playing?" he demanded accusingly.

Always a practical man, I was not going to have my expensively bought pleasure marred by doubt or fear.

I wrote George B. Parker, editor-in-chief of the Scripps-Howard Newspapers, though not in these exact words, to this effect:

"I'm having a wonderful time, but there's a man down here who says that a young fellow like me has no right to be staying on and on at this busy time of year. What do you say?"

He wrote back:

"A man who has carved out a newspaper with his bare hands has a right to do anything he pleases."

So I wrote my bank for a thousand dollars and returned to several more weeks of table d' hote dinners, cabana luncheons on the beach, and dancing in the night clubs. There was a companionship which might have led to marriage, but I drew back before that might have become imminent.

V

Knoxville Triumphs: Great Smoky
Mountains National Park and Council-
Manager Government—Retirement at
41?—The Move to Memphis—Purchase of
The Commercial Appeal—Proposal That
He Edit It and The Press-Scimitar

In the fall of 1931 a vacancy occurred in the editorship at
Memphis, due to Tom Sharp's being promoted to Buffalo. John
Sorrells, the executive editor of Scripps-Howard, wanted to fill
the vacancy by promoting the Memphis managing editor,
James K. Joyce, a skilled newspaper craftsman and delightful
personality, to the top job. I don't think John plainly told me
that, but I knew it from the way he said to me: "Bob and Roy
won't hear of anyone but you." Scripps-Howard owned *The
Press*, which our organization had started from scratch in 1906,
a year after Evansville was launched, and had bought the old
afternoon paper, *The News-Scimitar*. But the combination was
not doing anything like as well as the Knoxville combination.
So Bob Scripps and Roy Howard wanted me, because of my
success at Knoxville, to direct the editorial operation of the
important Memphis institution, *The Press-Scimitar*.

I did not want to leave Knoxville. My paper had become
the leading paper. We had been able to purchase *The Sentinel*,
the old afternoon paper, and thanks to the superb management
of Myron G. Chambers, in advertising and circulation we had
pulled far ahead of the morning paper. I liked the city, where I
had made good friends. I liked the mountains, where I spent
weekends. When I demurred at the suggestion that I move to
Memphis, Bob Scripps demanded:

"What do you want to do, stay here and get fat?"

The challenge settled it.

Despite my resistance to the change, I probably was ready for one.

For the previous winter, while I was spending a vacation in Nassau, I had had a strangely depressing, though brief, psychological experience. I had a sense of being finished. I actually inquired how much it would cost a retired person to live in Nassau. Think of it—to retire at 41! Later I was indignantly to wonder at the Navy's retiring people at that age.

(Editorial Column, The Memphis Press-Scimitar, January 4, 1954)

Nathan Schatz is a man I admire. He wisely found he couldn't retire.

For several years I bought fruit from him at his stand on Front Street. Fruit that is ripe, but not too ripe, is hard to find, but Mr. Schatz had it. He knew oranges, and he enjoyed supplying his customers with them.

Then one day I saw a diminishing supply on the usually well-laden stand. Mr. Schatz was selling out. "I am going to retire."

"Retire!" I repeated the word with astonishment and sadness. I knew I was going to miss Mr. Schatz and I believed he was going to miss the stand which he had operated for 43 years, sometimes with a cafe behind it.

Mr. Schatz spent "a miserable five months" at his comfortable home. He couldn't stand it. He missed the customers he loved and who loved him. He missed the beautiful piles of fruit. He reopened his stand.

Mr. Schatz is a pioneer. He is the first of many who will find that retirement is another one of these modern improvements that don't work.

Not every retired person has the means and the opportunity to go back into the business he left, as Mr. Schatz has. But many can find other occupations either in business or in civic work that will be really useful and give satisfaction and joy.

A few weeks later I heard my friend Dr. Henry Gotten, who is also a wise man, state the case against retirement in a speech to the Memphis Rotary Club.

Most people, he said, approach their declining years with no other thought than that once their responsibilities have lessened, they will have ample time "to fish, play golf, travel, or to sit on the front porch."

"Unfortunately," said Dr. Gotten, "when this time arrives, the individual may not be up to playing golf or fishing, his resources may not allow for travel, or his interest in these pursuits may have decreased. While it may seem very desirable to spend your declining years sitting on the front porch, a few months of such life will certainly bring depression, a sense of uselessness, and of futility.

"Elderly persons should engage in useful occupations or hobbies and any thought of retirement should not voluntarily be considered unless some other useful pursuit is available. One of the tragedies of our time is the forced retirement of individuals who are alert in mind, capable in body, have a wealth of experience and mature judgment which becomes useless to the individual and to society as a result thereof. Winston Churchill, Oliver Wendell Holmes and many others made great contributions to society long after the arbitrary retirement age of 65 was reached."

To sum up: Don't retire unless you must, and if you must, get another useful occupation, even though you are not paid for it in money. You will be paid for it in satisfaction.

By the time I left Knoxville for the new venture in Memphis, I felt that I was anything but finished. By coincidence, I left Knoxville ten years to the date from the time I entered the city—November 21, 1921 to November 21, 1931. They were ten happy years, fruitful in public service.

(From an address before the South Atlantic Regional meeting of the National Council of State Garden Clubs at Alexandria, La., in February, 1954. as reprinted in the Knoxville News-Sentinel.)

In 1921 as a young man I went to Knoxville to start a newspaper, The *Knoxville News*, for The Scripps-Howard organization. To find recreation after the arduous, though pleasing work of launching a new newspaper, on week ends I took a little coach on a logging railroad up into the Great Smoky Mountains where there was a summer resort at Elkmont. The railroad went up a gorge, and followed the course of the Little River, which tumbled clean and white-foamed over the great boulders which it had washed for centuries and aeons.

Across the stream one could see masses of rhododendron and laurel. Oak and pine and hemlock reached to the sky. I was amazed to find the climate and vegetation of Canada in the heart of the Sunny South.

DREAM COMES TRUE

IN THAT CITY was a lovely woman who had a dream. Men helped her to make it come true. The woman was Mrs. Willis Davis, wife of the manager of the Knoxville Iron Company. Mrs. Davis visited Elkmont. She saw those great peaks, the oldest things in this hemisphere, wrapped in the friendly mists that give them their name.

She saw their sides, clothed with trees and vegetation characteristic of the Southland at their base, and of Canada at their summit with those of all the intervening latitudes in between .. later we were to learn that the Smokies are a natural arboretum containing 130 species of native trees, 1300 kinds of flowering plants, and over 3600 plants of all kinds.

INSPIRATION FOR PARK

THEN MRS. DAVIS visited the national parks of the west, and said to her husband: "Beautiful as these parks are, they are no more wonderful than our own Smokies. Why can't we have a national park in the Great Smokies?" Never underestimate the power of a woman. That remark set her husband off on a course that led to the formation of the most popular of all our national parks—The Great Smoky Mountains National Park.

This is the story of ordinary human beings with faults and foibles who caught the vision of something great and grand outside themselves, devoted themselves to it and were made great and grand by their devotion to it.

STORY OF GREATNESS

SO I AM GOING to tell you of their foibles as well as their greatness, so you will not be discouraged from undertaking a project if you think you have foibles and faults and weaknesses, or deterred from working with other people who may come to you with some projects because you see their foibles, faults and weaknesses. I heard a friend say of Willis Davis:

"Willis loves to hear the sound of his own voice." If that was a fact, it was a good thing. For Willis began talking about the Great Smokies and how they should be set aside as a national park.

CAMPBELL IRRITATED

CARLOS C. CAMPBELL was then assistant secretary of the Knoxville Chamber of Commerce, of which Mr. Davis was a member of the board of directors. Mr. Campbell relates that he was considerably irritated by hearing Mr. Davis rave about the Smokies. He says Mr. Davis bored people.

Let us not hesitate to bore people with our enthusiasms, if we must; let us try not to be bored by the enthusiasm of others, but rather to see their visions and catch their enthusiasms, and join with them in making the great dream come true.

Carlos C. Campbell did not remain irritated and bored long. He caught the enthusiasm of Willis Davis and became the best informed man on the Great Smoky Mountains, and the most understanding, courageous and persistent friend the park project, and later the park itself, has ever had.

MONUMENTS TO FAITH

MR. CAMPBELL has since said that of all the indispensable things without which the park movement could not have achieved success, first and foremost, "was Willis Davis' application of his implicit Christian Science faith to the park movement."

Without faith, we can do nothing. With faith, we can surmount seemingly insurmountable difficulties. The Great Smoky Mountains National Park stands today as a perpetual monument to the faith of Willis Davis.

It takes all kinds of people to make a world, thank God, and it takes all kinds of people to make a project. So welcome them all to your project.

CHAPMAN WAS LEADER

DAVID C. CHAPMAN was a very different man from Willis Davis. Willis Davis was a gentle, courtly, white-haired man. If Willis Davis was the inspiring priest of the movement, Dave Chapman was its leader and commanding officer who directed the ever-increasing forces in the strategy and battles in the cause which so often seemed hopeless to a final complete triumph.

In contrast with the spiritual Willis Davis, Dave Chapman was a worldly man. He had jousted in those tournaments in which the South revives medieval chivalry. He was a war veteran.

Hepburn Saunders and Dave Chapman married sisters. I heard the story, which may be apocryphal, that Mr. Saunders sarcastically remarked of their father-in-law:

"The Colonel is very fortunate in his sons-in-law. From the two of them he can find out anything he wants to know. For Dave knows everything except that he is a damn fool, and I know that."

KNOWING AND SHREWD

DAVE SURELY had self-confidence, and he was a ready talker. He may even have been a bit on the egotistical side.

If so, it was all to the good of the park project, for difficult tasks take self-confidence, which is the next best thing to the kind of faith Willis Davis had. But he was not a damn fool, he was intelligent, knowing and shrewd.

The qualities which Dave Chapman did not have, he acquired. It is a delightful thing to watch a plant grow, or a tree grow. It is even more delightful, it is inspiring, to watch a man or a woman grow. I watched Dave Chapman grow.

WANTED A ROAD

IN THE BEGINNING as a wholesale drug merchant, he was only one of those materialistic business men who thought of the Great Smokies as nothing more than a barrier that interfered with the free flow of business between North Carolina and Tennessee.

He got into this thing because he wanted a road to surmount the barrier. In the beginning he would not have cared if that road had so opened the wilderness to development that a park would have become impossible.

But Dave Chapman caught the vision of Willis Davis of the glory that might be. He listened to the naturalists and park experts and idealists from all over America who got interested in saving the Great Smokies, and he became an idealist himself.

LEARNS BIG LESSON

THE WORDS "flora and fauna" in many a speech and interview tripped readily from a tongue which had been given to the less-learned conversation of the cocktail hours.

He started out trying to build a road, yet he learned what all conservationists know, that while you have to have certain roads to make a nature area accessible, it is just as important to keep them out of other areas, and large areas at that, if we are to preserve our irreplaceable wilderness.

How appropriate it is that a highway and a mountain are named for him. Too much honor cannot be given his memory. I remember Dave Chapman with affection and admiration as a man who showed how a man whose life seems to have reached its limits can expand his outlook, his mind and his personality, can grow, and reach heights the associates of his youth would not have predicted.

TASK SEEMS IMPOSSIBLE

YET DAVE CHAPMAN, for all the idealism into which he grew, fortunately remained the man of the world who knew what made things tick, and a tough fighter.

It seemed impossible, because a national park had never before been created. The great parks of the West had simply been set aside, out of lands which were, and had always been, public lands. It wasn't hard to do. But the lands out of which the Great Smoky Mountains National Park was to be made, if it was to be made, were all in private ownership, and there were many owners. They didn't want to sell, and if they did, where was the money coming from?

DONATION REQUIRED

FURTHERMORE the National Park Service had a strict rule that all lands for a national park had to be donated, not acquired by congressional appropriation. They did this so that lands unworthy of national park status would not be wished on them through politics.

This situation called for a long and hard campaign that started in 1923 and did not end until 1940, when the park was dedicated. The public had to be aroused and brought to one mind on the importance of the project to the region. Donations had to be sought, legislators, governors, senators and philanthropists persuaded. Enemies and rivals had to be defeated.

DARK HOURS PASSED

CRISIS followed crisis, battle followed battle, and there was many a dark hour between the shining victories.

I will relate only a few.

While the project was being launched in Knoxville to make a national park of the Great Smokies, there was a parallel movement in Washington to locate a national park somewhere in the East. The Southern Appalachian National Park Commission was named.

But they were reluctant even to look at the Great Smokies, so remote and little known they were. They seemed to favor better known areas.

PHOTOGRAPHS SHOW BEAUTY

THE COMMITTEE had a meeting slated at Asheville to consider another area. An agreement was wrung from them that if the proponents of the Smokies would come to Asheville, they would get a hearing. Here the indispensable photographer entered the picture.

The photographs, taken by James E. Thompson, Knoxville photographer, showed the beauties of the Smokies and aroused the interest of the commission. Two members of the commission agreed to inspect the area.

On a trip up rugged, roadless, unspoiled Mt. LeConte, the commissioners were won over. The Smokies need only to be seen, and the sun shone that day, and they were seen.

ORDER REVERSED

THE COMMISSION recommended two national parks, Shenandoah and Great Smoky. They put Shenandoah as the first, because of its nearness to the center of population. The public has reversed that order. The public puts Great Smoky first, Shenandoah second.

During the travel year 1953–1954 Great Smoky attracted more visitors than any other national park, 2,250,772. Shenandoah was second with 1,673,346 [Editor's Note: by the early '70s, visitors to the Great Smokies park reached an annual figure of more than 8,000,000].

Legislation was passed in 1926 approving the park in Tennessee and North Carolina if the money could be raised.

MORE POLITICAL PLANK

AUSTIN PEAY made the park a plank in his platform and was elected governor of Tennessee. The first step was to get an appropriation for the purchase of the tract of the Little River Lumber Co., on which logging was actively under way. Mrs. Willis P. Davis, mother of the park, now a member of the Legislature, was given the honor of introducing the bill.

It wasn't easy to pass the bill. The park movement met a powerful and tireless enemy, James B. Wright, attorney, who wanted the area to be not a national park, but a national forest, under which timber cutting and other economic activities would be permitted.

LEGISLATORS TAKE LOOK

THE CHAMBER of Commerce felt it necessary to raise a special fund of $5,000 to bring the entire Legislature to Knoxville in a special train to see the Smokies. The bill passed, 58 to 36. The city council of Knoxville donated one-third of the $273,557 purchase price of the first block of land for the park.

There followed a giant joint campaign for funds by the Great Smoky Mountains Conservation Association of Tennessee and the North Carolina Park Commission.

A professional fund-raising firm was employed. In the dollars of businessmen and the pennies of school children, nearly $400,000 was raised in each state.

MONEY VOTED

THEN NORTH CAROLINA took the lead. North Carolina's Legislature in 1927 voted $2,000,000 for land purchases if Tennessee would match it. Tennessee did. The land Tennessee had already acquired was valued at $500,000, and an additional $1,500,000 was voted.

But another $5,000,000 was needed? Where to get it?

Arno B. Cammerer, at that time assistant director of the National Park Service, was given a leave of absence to see if he could find that money. Find it he did.

ROCKEFELLER DONATES

HE WENT TO that great American family whose members have shown us that we need to have rich people to make our democracy work and that we need to have rich people who think, live and act as the members of that family do—the great Rockefeller family. John D. Rockefeller, Jr. secretly visited the Great Smokies, was awed by what he termed their "indescribable beauty," and pleased by what he called "the immaculate cleanliness" of a mountaineer's humble home, that of Willie Myers in Cades' Cove, which he visited.

GIFT IS $5,000,000

HE GAVE the word which resulted in a gift of $5,000,000 from the trustees of the Laura Spelman Rockefeller Fund which had been set up as a memorial to his mother.

There was many a legal, political, and even physical combat ahead, but at last the dream of a woman, and the project of the men her dream inspired to action, came to complete fulfillment. The Great Smoky Mountains National Park stands today, 505,000 acres of perpetual natural beauty.

Part of it is a wilderness area, never to be penetrated by road, automobile, airplane or other modern invention.

What part did our Scripps-Howard newspaper, The Knoxville *News-Sentinel* have in all this?

THE EDITOR sat in the councils of the park movement and went with them on the field trips. We reported the news, the activities of the citizens working for the park, accurately and zestfully. We played it up. When a crisis arose, we played that up.

When enemies struck at the park project, we hit back with hammer blows on our editorial page. We praised the citizens who were working so unselfishly. When skulduggery was afoot, we turned on a revealing light. We exposed the machinations of the chief foe of the park movement, Attorney James B. Wright.

TIMBER RIGHTS RESERVED

UNFORTUNATELY, when the state purchased the 76,000 acres of the Little River Lumber Co. land in 1926, the company was permitted to retain timber-cutting rights, although it was stipulated that it could not cut or destroy any timber under 10 inches in diameter. Timber-cutting rights were limited to 15 years.

It was a shock when, early in 1929, following many rumors, it was discovered that the company had ruined, and was continuing to ruin, for generations to come, some of the finest virgin timber in the tract the state had purchased.

Numerous efforts were made to induce the company to quit cutting the fine timber or to change its timbering methods so as to conserve the timber under 10 inches, and the smaller growing trees.

PUBLIC HORRIFIED

THE NEWS-SENTINEL in 1929, sent a reporter, John T. Moutoux, and a photographer in an airplane over the tract to take pictures of the ruin. These pictures, published Sunday, Feb. 10, 1929, horrified the public.

They showed entire mountainsides despoiled, the trees virtually all down or denuded of their limbs and tops. All were masses of debris. The company had been using for nearly two years a monster known as a skidder in its operations.

This engine of destruction, in getting logs down hillsides, destroyed all timber in its path. The mountainsides and valleys between looked as if they had been struck by barrages of artillery in war.

AGREEMENT REACHED

INSTANTLY, there arose the demand, louder than ever, that something be done to stop this despoliation. There was much talk of a suit for an injunction.

Arbitration of the value of the reserved timber rights was proposed. But this proposal covered only timber lying outside the Middle Prong of Little River, which was a comparatively small part of the whole. Colonel W.B. Townsend, head of the Little River Lumber Co., was agreeable to arbitration.

An agreement was reached whereby A.B. Cammerer, of the U.S. Interior Department, and D.H. Tipton, of Little River Lumber Co., were to set the line outside of which Colonel Townsend would sell timber rights to the park commission, at a price to be fixed by another arbitrating body.

5000 ACRES SAVED

MEANWHILE, a bill was placed in Legislature to give the park board condemnation rights to acquire what it wanted. Cammerer said the agreement would save much valuable timber. By the compromise 5000 acres were saved.

Meanwhile, there appeared in the 1929 Legislature a bill to provide for enlargement of the park board from seven to 18 members. It gave Governor Henry Horton power to appoint the new board, and made Horton and two of his cabinet members of the board. It seemed skulduggery was afoot. Colonel D.C. Chapman's enemies, it was believed, were behind the bill, and in the far background could be seen the face of J.B. Wright.

INIMICAL ACT KILLED

THIS BILL WOULD place control of the park board and of all future park policy under control of the Horton Administration. It stirred anger all over East Tennessee among friends of the park movement. Telegrams protesting passage of the bill poured into Horton and the Legislature by the thousands.

A few days after the introduction of the bill, the Rockefeller interests, who had donated $5,000,000 to help establish the park, dropped a boulder on this bill. The Rockefellers asked that action on the bill be delayed.

Governor Horton replied he saw no reason why it could not be delayed, and added that he saw no reason for enlarging the commission. The bill failed to pass.

FUND BILL EXPOSED

IN THE SAME Legislature of 1929 a bill was introduced to provide that all park funds should be deposited in the State Treasury, including funds certified from the Rockefeller gift. This was analyzed by a *News-Sentinel* staff correspondent. The exposure prevented its passage.

Had it passed, the whole park project might have blown up, for later the State of Tennessee, controlled by the manipulators Lea and Caldwell, deposited state funds in Caldwell's Bank of Tennessee. That bank failed. What if the park funds had been in it?

PAPER GIVEN CREDIT

YES, OUR NEWSPAPER did a lot. Yet it was no more than a newspaper ought to do. When citizens work for the public, they are volunteers. They do it over and above their regular occupations. But public service is the daily business of a newspaper.

So I was surprised when Arno B. Cammerer, by now director of the National Park Service, after the triumph of the park movement, thanked me with tears in his eyes. "Without the *News-Sentinel* we couldn't have done it," he said.

I have learned since that a newspaper can often serve as the indispensable half of a civic project. The citizens are the other half.

(Editorial Page article, The Memphis Press-Scimitar, December 1954.)

Council-manager government is proposed for Memphis.

Advocates for this form of government point to the many cities in which it has succeeded—Richmond, Cincinnati, Kansas City, Dallas, Fort Worth and hundreds of others.

Sometimes they are asked: "But how about Knoxville?"

They have heard bad reports of governmental affairs in Knoxville. What happened in Knoxville?

I can tell the story. I was editor of *The Knoxville News*— later *The News-Sentinel*—when council-manager was adopted there in 1923. I saw it in operation. I have frequently visited Knoxville since I left that city in 1931 and have kept in touch with developments up to the present.

Knoxville had the commission form. It became inefficient and corrupt and broke down. A citizens movement brought council-manager government. Leading citizens, including the city's most successful business and professional men and a labor leader, were drafted to compose the council. This council engaged as city manager the most capable man they could find: Louis Brownlow, who as then manager of Petersburg, Virginia, and president of the City Managers Association. He had previously been police commissioner of Washington, D.C. under Woodrow Wilson.

Brownlow thought the best was none too good for Knoxville, though it then was a city of less than 80,000 people. He boldly hired the welfare director of the State of Virginia, Frank Bane, to be welfare director of Knoxville. He got Major Otey Walker, a high class man, to be safety commissioner. Bane got a trained man to be health officer. The city hospital, which had been a scandal under the commission form of government, with awful neglect of patients, was cleaned up and became the city's pride. Long-needed major improvements were made—streets and sewers, a fine new waterworks built, a new city hall acquired, a new bridge over the Tennessee River planned which was later built. Yet despite these large expenditures, the cost of government was actually reduced. High salaries (for the time) were paid—Brownlow himself got $15,000. But these officials earned their salaries many times over by the graft, waste and inefficiency which they eliminated.

A Citizens Charter Committee drafted candidates for council and won election after election. They enjoyed making politics a matter of citizenship. Councilmen enjoyed giving their community honored service. City employees enjoyed doing a good job without interference of politics.

Knoxville had the finest municipal government in the United States at that time.

It wasn't all peaches and cream. There was a small minority on the council which was not in sympathy with the new government. There were a few disgruntled politicians who for reasons of personal pique or self-interest did all they could to hurt the administration and the citizens movement which backed it. But their destructive efforts would have been to no avail had there not been a change in the newspaper situation.

All three newspapers warmly supported council-manager government in the beginning. When the three were reduced to two by the consolidation of the *News* and *Sentinel*, there was still unanimity.

Then the morning paper, the *Journal,* was acquired by Luke Lea, the Nashville promoter. To Luke Lea, a newspaper was not a business of purveying news and an institution of public service, it was an instrument to be used in pursuing his political and personal schemes. He could not use a non-political council-manager government, so he proceeded to try to break it down. His newspaper harassed the government and the citizens who were sponsoring it and encouraged the politicians who were opposed to it. At the show of real opposition, some citizens lost courage and quit. At this point, let Loye W. Miller, present editor of the *News-Sentinel,* pick up the story:

"For a good many years, council-manager government withstood this attack. But finally the politicians began to succeed. They elected some councilmen who were not the broad-minded, public-spirited citizens that Knoxville had become accustomed to. They regarded the manager's job as a political plum. Politicians instead of men trained in public administration were selected by Council as city manager. Council meetings became noisy political forums with little effort being given to develop a long-range policy and program.

"The few councilmen of ability and with the proper conception of manager type of government found themselves under constant attack.

"They would not have minded this, and would have continued to serve, and fight to win, if there had been a successful citizens movement to back them up. But the citizens movement which started so hopefully failed to form a firm, permanent organization which is necessary to protect good government and good public servants. Such organizations are responsible for the success of council-manager government in hundreds of American cities, notably Cincinnati. When the citizens movement in Knoxville withered away, do did their good government.

"Knoxville citizens, remembering the glory of the fine nonpolitical government they once had, sought to recapture it.

They formed the Good Government Group. In the membership were men and women who were able and civic-minded. But they were timid, afraid of the politicians, and made some early mistakes which terrified them. The organization did not live long.

"Contributing to the sabotage of city manager government were a succession of delegations to the Legislature representing Knox County that every two years tampered and experimented with Knoxville's government. Knoxville's charter probably has been amended by the Legislature more times than that of any other Tennessee city. Each time the excuse was that the community was in an uproar and the amendments were designed to achieve peace. Actually, the motives were always political, to transfer power from one faction to another.

(Council-manager government could not be legislated out in Tennessee today, since constitutional amendments have been adopted against the ripper bills and providing for home rule.)

"In 1937, the manager form was abolished by legislative act and the strong mayor-council form enacted. There was a moment of public rebellion, and the people elected as mayor a candidate who pledged to perform as a manager and who promised to work for restoration of the manager charter. This was done two years later, but public interest died down again, and in 1947, the manager charter was again repealed and the strong mayor form re-enacted. It is still in force.

"Politicians are now in full control, and there is constant warfare between the mayor and the dominant faction in City Council. The city's debt continues to grow in spite of an annual revenue of about $11,000,000; the bonded debt is now about $25,000,000.

"The most tragic result of this sort of factional, political strife is that the citizens are suspicious and dissatisfied. Community spirit cannot thrive in such an atmosphere. When affairs are administered expertly and in a business-like fashion by those trained in the work, there is public respect and confidence.

"The conclusion to be arrived at from the Knoxville experience, I think, is that public complacency and disinterest are dangerous to good government. The people must actively and vigorously support good public servants and protect them from unwarranted attack. When such co-operation exists there is harmony, community spirit and progress. Without it, good government disappears."

To sum up:

Knoxville had the commission form of government. It failed. Knoxville turned to council-manager government. It succeeded brilliantly. But citizens didn't know how to support it and let designing politicians take it away from them. Now Knoxville has the strong-mayor form. It is better than the commission form which preceded council-manager government, but it is far inferior to the council-manager government which Knoxville at one time operated so successfully.

The moral:

Council-manager is the best form of government. It works superbly when citizens work it. But even the finest piece of mechanism requires the attention of capable operators. Good government is not automation.

When he bade me godspeed from Knoxville to the new field in Memphis Bob Scripps said to me:

"I want you in the general management. I like what you did for the people in Knoxville. But you will have to succeed in more than one city."

I never did get in the general management. I would never have wanted any responsibility for financial administration, though I do think my sense of values, even in financial matters, could have been depended on. A few years later when we acquired *The Commercial Appeal* Bob Scripps proposed that I, as senior editor in the city, determine the policy of both papers. I declined. I did not want to be hobbled by the pre-Civil War tradition of *The Commercial Appeal*. However, had I shown any interest I think that John Sorrells, born in Pine Bluff, and worshipper of *The Commercial Appeal* from boyhood, would have dissuaded Bob from that course. He would have realized how impractical it would have been to give a person of my convictions and temperament direct responsibility for *The Commercial Appeal*. Of indirect responsibility I proved fully capable. I worked closely with John to persuade our associates that our operation of *The CA* should be undertaken with the greatest respect for its tradition, and for what its subscribers wanted it to be; I had no little influence in this direction. I was entrusted with writing Scripps-Howard's announcement of the purchase of *The Commercial Appeal* and of the concern's policy with regard to that influential newspaper.

Bob Scripps later invited me to take a voyage with him on his yacht. I loved my work so much and was so reluctant to leave it that I showed little interest in the invitation and it was never made specific as to date. Later I was to recognize that my interest in my job was so extreme as to amount, from a spiritual standpoint, to idolatry.

Bob Scripps died young. Whether he would ever have carried out his earlier wish to have me in the general management I will never know.

VI

The Memphis Years: 17-Year Crusade against Crump Machine and For Democracy—The Rule of Fear—"Citizens Can Beat Politicians at Their Own Game," and in 1948, They Do—The End of the Crump Dictatorship

I entered Knoxville with confidence in a formula to assure me success. I needed no formula to give me confidence that I would succeed in Memphis. The fact that both Scripps and Howard would hear of no one else for the position of Memphis editor was enough to convince me that success in Knoxville would assure success in Memphis. I entered the new field, if anything, over-confident, perhaps even vain, cocky. But I succeeded well enough.

Before leaving Knoxville I asked a wise woman friend: "You know me and you know Memphis. What advice do you have for me?"

"Memphis loves to play. You do not play enough. Play!"

(Letter to Miss Gertrude Meeman, November, 1931.)

Dear Gertrude:

This is the end of a very happy week of auspicious beginning. I could not have been introduced to Memphis under more favorable circumstances.

The paper here is strong and universally liked. Eveyone welcomes me so cordially and hospitably. Instead of greeting me as a "foreigner" they greet me as a valued new citizen. They all say what the mayor said in a speech: "We hope he'll like us." I do like them immensely. I am tremendously enjoying the free metropolitan atmosphere. Memphis is a joyous city. Everybody has a good time or tries to, and I haven't met a kill-joy yet.

I have had to speak at a luncheon and a dinner and over the

radio, all of which is new to me, but I'll have to get used to it. . . . Unless the country goes to smash, I will succeed here. After looking the situation over, I am certain of it. *The one thing we cannot afford to be is cheap. So throw away all the junk before you come.* Believe me when I say that the slightest bit of cheapness or bad taste will cost me plenty of money. We are starting a new experience. We both know what is right; let's have the courage to do it in everything. It may be desirable to get an apartment, as there are lots of burglars in Memphis. I'll examine everything. Write me at once about when you want to come so I can make plans. I suppose it is settled that the Stongs[1] do not want the house.

Living at Hotel Peabody is almost as good as the Pancoast (I even get tomato jelly). I am really on vacation, get lots of sleep and my work is all pleasure. You have a good time and take it easy too—there's no harm.

With love,
Ed

Memphis does indeed love to play. At the time I went there the love of play submerged the serious interests that are also there. I took the advice and accepted most of the social invitations that came to me. And since people want to know a newspaper editor the invitations were many—dinners, cocktail parties, dances, debut parties. Much later I was to adopt the saving plan of not making two engagements for a night out in succession. I should have done it in the beginning. This is a good rule for anyone, no matter how young. "Go home much," says Emerson.

While I was thus doing society, I justified it on the ground that it helped my work thus to get around, to get acquainted, to hear what people are saying, to find out what is going on. To some extent this was true. But, with the best intentions, I carried it too far. Doing society became too much of a good thing.

Here is one example of the value of society in a newspaperman's experience. At a small dinner when there is general conversation, people talk very freely say what they think

---

[1]Ben Stong, brother of Phil Stong, the novelist, had succeeded Meeman at Knoxville.

and tell what they know. At such a dinner, Dr. Russell Hen-
nessy, a physician, told how the Rev. Israel H. Noe, dean of the
Episcopal Cathedral, a theological non-conformist, was engaged in a fast to prove that man can live without matter. He
had conducted a mission at Knoxville when I was editor there,
and I had editorially commended him. He later told me this
commendation had given him the courage to advocate openly
what he believed. In gratitude for this he had become my
lifelong friend. Later he had been the object of a sensational
divorce suit in which his wife charged he had given up conjugal
relations. Now, this fast. The Episcopal church feared he
would die, but did not know what to do. I decided to break
the story. It was a wise decision. I think the publication of the
situation led to the measures which saved his life.

Dean Noe was an extremist. Some of his ideas were odd,
indeed, but he was sincere, good, and truly spiritual, and his
effect on normal people was good. God rest his soul.

I could hardly have received a more hospitable welcome,
or been accepted more cordially, or treated with more respect
than I was in Memphis. But it irked me to think that people
didn't know what I had accomplished in Knoxville, both in
journalism and public service; that I had to prove myself all
over again. Did that feeling show that I was spoiled, egotistical,
expected too much? Certainly.

I opposed the E.H. Crump political machine as a crusading editor committed not only to upholding democracy, but to
improving it, was bound to do. In this I became associated with
the Voters League, which consisted mostly of followers of
former Governor Malcolm Patterson, Southerners of the old
school. They opposed the Crump machine for the reasons I
did, and for one that I did not share with them, that he made
voters of Negroes, though we agreed in hating the Crump
method of voting them in truckloads, as mere pawns.

(Editorial from The Knoxville News-Sentinel, May 8, 1931.)

Independent and patriotic citizens of Tennessee feel
genuine concern lest Congressman Edward H. Crump, who for

years has made a farce of Memphis elections, and affected the
state elections thereby, shall obtain an increase in influence in
state affairs. They fear that he will obtain such an increase in
influence if Governor Horton is impeached and Speaker Scott
Fitzhugh of Memphis succeeds Horton.

But partners in crime of Luke Lea and Rogers Caldwell and
beneficiaries of the Horton administration are only pretending
when they act horrified at the prospect of Crump rule. They
were not horrified at Crump in 1929. Then they sought and got
Crump's aid in putting through the funding board legislation at
the special session by which the looters made it possible for
them to concentrate state funds in their banks, so they could
"borrow" it. They sought and got Crump's aid in re-electing
Horton while their banks were tottering. Had the result been
close, Crump's herded and manipulated vote might have been
the cause of Horton's re-election.

The evil character of the Crump political practices and of
his influence to the state have not been exaggerated. Crump is
the foe of democracy and good government. If Crump had never
done anything worse than give assistance to the Lea-Caldwell
gang in the special session and support Governor Horton for
re-election afterward, he would merit eternal banishment from
the politics of Tennessee. However, the danger of Crump
domination of the state has been much exaggerated. It should be
remembered that Tammany Hall has never been able to control
the state of New York, though New York City is more important
relatively in New York state than Memphis is in Tennessee.

Because Crump is bad, does it follow that the people of
Tennessee should spare Horton lest Crump gain strength?

By no means!

Through the office of Governor Henry Horton has been
perpetrated against the people of Tennessee one of the most
gigantic crimes in American history. Millions of dollars of the
people's money has been turned to private use, and in the chain
of resulting events, people have lost their life's savings and men
have committed suicide. If Horton did not have a guilty knowledge of what has gone on, he must be deemed mentally incom-
petent. If Horton had a guilty knowledge, he should be removed. If he had no guilty knowledge, he is so mentally weak
that it is dangerous to leave the helm of the ship of state in his
hands. In either case Horton should go.

"But what of Crump?" What of Crump, indeed!

If the people of Tennessee show themselves to be so indifferent to wrong-doing, so weak of will, so faint of heart that they will allow the great Lea-Caldwell crime to go unpunished and unrebuked, and allow its principal instrument to keep on sitting in the governor's chair, when the evidence is all so plain and practically undisputed, then what hope can they have of being strong enough to keep Crump from running over the state?

But if the people of Tennessee rise in their might, and inflict condign punishment on Lea and Caldwell, and remove Horton, then they will be saying: "All right, Mr. Crump! You didn't steal any money. But you made a political alliance with this gang, you helped them get the laws they want, and you threw an election in Memphis for them. We're cleaning up Tennessee. You stay in your own bailiwick, and you'd better watch your step even there. Memphis people may not be tired of it, but the rest of the state is tired of waiting for returns from Shelby County's herded and manipulated vote before they know whom they have chosen for governor. Watch your step!"

That would mean something to Crump.

If the people of Tennessee let Horton get away with it, the gentlemen from Memphis would have a right to laugh long and loud and say:

"Boys, the people of this state seem to like to be walked on. Let's walk on 'em."

We must get rid of Horton first; then deal with Crump. With the exercise the civic muscles of Tennessee would get in making a thorough clean-up of the Lea-Caldwell gang, disposal of the Crump outfit should be comparatively easy.

As for Speaker Fitzhugh, no one knows what kind of a governor he will make. It is not certain he will bow to Crump. It is quite possible he will make a good governor. Good or bad, is he likely to be worse than Horton?

If Fitzhugh should go wrong, it will be easy to dispose of him if a precedent has been set by not letting Horton get away with it.

There is no hope for progress or even holding our own, if Horton remains in the governor's chair [Editor's Note: He did. Neither impeached nor willing to resign, Governor Horton served out his term]

(Editorial from The Memphis Press-Scimitar, 1932.)

The organization of the Voters' League is one of the most hopeful things that has happened in Shelby County in years.

In John M. Dean this organization has a wise and able leader.

The Voters' League will be most effective if its members do not think of it as having as its main purpose a fight on Crump and Crumpism.

If Memphis had always had a strong non-partisan Voters' League, Crumpism would never have been able to fasten its ugly grip on this city.

The growth and success of such a Voters' League will mean the end of Crumpism.

But Crumpism, after being put out of power, is more likely to stay dead if the Voters' League has pursued all the activities which such an organization of the people should pursue, the elimination of Crumpism being a mere by-product of such civic activities.

If the Voters' League became merely a factional political organization out to get Crump, its success would not free the county, for it would result only in another political machine taking its place.

But if it practices fundamental principles of modern popular government, it will have built a structure of democracy in which the present bossism, coercion and corruption will have no place.

The Voters' League should see that two kinds of undesirable members are excluded.

It should exclude those suspected of being agents or spies of the county organization. The civic clubs once had possibilities of being true organizations of the people, strong enough to cope with the politicians. But the machine packed them with its henchmen and they soon became impotent.

It should exclude those who are mere soreheads, who are against the county organization only because they are not in it, but would use the same kind of corrupt methods as Crumpism used if they had the chance.

(News story from The Memphis Press-Scimitar, 1932.)

The aim of the political machine is not to make democracy work, but to work democracy, Edward J. Meeman, editor of *The Press-Scimitar*, told members of the Voters' League at their regular luncheon at Lowenstein's Friday.

Meeman praised the physical accomplishments of the Crump machine in respect to viaducts, subways, street improvements, parks and playgrounds, but condemned it for its reign by fear and its suppression of the rights of the people to think and vote as they choose.

"My dentist complained the other day," said Meeman, "that it is hard to get the people to take as much interest in their teeth as the dentist does."

TO PRESERVE RIGHTS

"A newspaper editor likes to see the people take as much interest in their rights as the newspaper does. An organization such as the Voters' League will preserve and keep in working order the rights of the people—their teeth.

"Just as teeth suffer for the lack of use, so the rights of the people will decay if they are not used.

"An organization like this and an independent newspaper can accomplish much in a city. It is the business of the newspaper to dig up and print the news. It can interpret and comment on it in the editorial columns, but it cannot take action.

"It is the business of such organizations as the Voters' League to act—to make democracy work.

"To make democracy work is to make America work, for America stands supremely for democracy.

NO BETTER SOCIETY

"There can be no better form of society than democracy. It is useless to turn to other forms, for one cannot turn to them without turning backward. There is only one way to go forward and that is to perfect democracy, to make democracy work better than it does.

"Today we hear much about our technical development and mass production, but let us not be sure that all this technical advancement could have been made had it not been for the political democracy which made for equality of opportunity and for a spirit of initiative and invention.

"Democracy comes from two Greek words—"people" and "rule of". Democracy means the right of the people to rule—literally.

"In American democracy there has grown up an institution known as the political machine. This is not an institution to make democracy work, but to work democracy.

MINORITY RULES

"By using public offices, groups of men get together and plan to stick together as a minority to take advantage of the majority—and not be too scrupulous about it—not to be too careful about the rights of the people.

"We have such a machine in Memphis. Let us, however, be fair. In some respects it stands well above the average city machine. The Memphis machine has produced a higher degree of efficiency in office than the average machine. It has had a better program in meeting the physical needs of the people than most machines.

"But no machine has gone so far to deny the people the right to their own opinions of measures and men and to vote those opinions; no machine has gone so far to establish a rule of fear.

MUCH TO BE PROUD OF

"We have much to be proud of it Memphis. We often forget the physical progress we have made. Under Crump more progress was made in eliminating grade crossings than in any other American City. Started under Crump and reaching its full success under Mayor Paine, our city planning accomplishments were rated the greatest in America, and Memphis is pointed to by experts as an example to other cities. We have splendid parks and playgrounds, an efficient health department and good schools.

"We have straightened streets and removed bad spots. We should be proud of all these, but—'For what is a man profited if he shall gain the whole world and lose his own soul?' What does it profit Memphis to have all these splendid physical accomplishments and have not freedom of mind and freedom of spirit? It is fine for the children to go to our parks and playgrounds and fill their lungs with fresh, clean air.

"But we will not have done right by these children unless we let them breathe the air of freedom.

"We have provided splendid school buildings for the boys and girls, but we will not have done right by them if we let them be taught by teachers who are in fear."

MACHINE IS "IMMORAL"

Meeman said that while the Memphis machine had accomplished many things, it is immoral and wrong in that it had used public employees against the people who employed and paid them, but that it has avoided public scandals of misappropriated funds, of bribing by contractors and the selling of franchises—things that have occurred under machines in other cities.

"While credit is due for this, yet machine rule can give no guarantee that it will not happen in the future, and can give no guarantee against change in leadership," he said.

"It is up to us to abolish the machine before it costs what it is bound to cost," he continued. "It is already costing us much in the way of duplicated costs of government.

ONLY ONE SUBSTITUTE

"There can be only one substitute for the machine and that is organizations of people that will make it their business to make democracy work.

"What is everybody's business is nobody's business. There must be groups of people who think what they please, who will bring their purposes before the people, be assured of the right to vote for or against them, and be assured that they have the right to have that vote honestly counted.

"To my mind, Thomas Jefferson was the greatest man this country ever produced. He never lost faith in democracy, but he also believed in aristocracy—not in the way the word is often misused, not in the aristocracy of wealth—that is plutocracy— not in the aristocracy of family—that is feudalism—but in aristocracy—the rule of the best, the rule of wisdom and virtue.

"In order to make democracy work we must bring about a government of wisdom and virtue. This can only be done by organizations of this kind—a cutting across of all parties, a cutting across of various economic views."

Meeman said Memphis did not enjoy the friendship and respect of the rest of the state as it deserved—"not because it has falsely been represented, but because the truth has been told."

The Voters' League failed. It was the last organized opposition to the Crump machine, and the machine evolved into something worse than a machine, into a local dictatorship, not to be broken until 1948, and I was to have the rare experience of operating a free press under a totalitarian dictatorship, which controlled nearly everything in town,—not only the politics and government, but the Bar Association, the Parent-Teacher Association, the Council of Civic Clubs, the American Legion, the labor unions, the business community.

(Editorial from The Memphis Press-Scimitar, Novemeber, 1939.)

WE CHOOSE A MAYOR

We now know who "Mr. Blank" is.

We now know the identity of the man whom leading supporters of the Shelby County political organization underwrote, though they did not know who he was when they signed mayoralty nominating petitions in blank the other day in an act of blind faith.

Technically, it is E. H. Crump, who is to run for the office, but actually it is Walter Chandler, who is to take the mayor's office after he has voted for repeal of the arms embargo in Washington.

And what do the people think of this method of choosing their city government?

From the expressions we have heard, they don't like the process that gives them no part in choosing their mayor, that even leaves them in the dark as to who is being chosen for them until the very eve of "election." They feel some civic embarrassment that a city of 280,000 people should have allowed things to drift into such a condition.

But this indefensible and unpopular method of choice could hardly have selected a more popular man than Walter Chandler. Undoubtedly he is well and favorably known personally and his public record is generally approved. He made an intelligent, hard-working and efficient city attorney and congressman. In Congress his record was mostly good—except for such a significant exception as his vote against the Hatch bill.

Whether Mr. Chandler will make a good mayor remains to be seen. He has had little if any executive experience, and his qualifications in the field of administration are unknown and unproved.

He is quite subservient to the machine. If there are limits to that subservience they have not been reached. If there is even a faint spark of independence we have not seen it. He was put in the doghouse by the machine without the slightest justification, yet he never complained. He is being moved from Congress, where, from the standpoint of the machine and from the standpoint of most citizens, he has made good and where he is happy, to a mayoralty where he may not be happy, again without complaint. It is not in the nature of things that such "yessing" makes for good government—to say nothing of democracy.

Is the political organization so poor in material that it must rob Congress of a man suited to his job there because there is no other man in the organization good enough to be mayor?

It is the political exigencies of the machine, its need of an acceptable candidate, and not the need of good government in Memphis, which compelled the removal of Walter Chandler from the congressional seat, where he and most other citizens preferred that he stay, to the mayoralty.

For better municipal government than we now have, unmenaced by political maneuverings, could be obtained if we had the NONPOLITICAL COUNCIL-MANAGER SYSTEM in Memphis.

This form is in successful use in more than 500 American cities.

Under that form, citizens nominate outstanding citizens for the council. They do not have to leave their business or profession to serve. It is the highest honor that can come to a citizen. There is no dirty "politics" in it. They do not have to leave their private business to serve on the council, for the actual work of administration is done by city employees, who are directed by a city manager, who has made a profession of municipal service. The city manager in turn appoints the other city employees on a merit basis with the approval of the citizen council. You get democracy thru the citizen council; you get efficiency thru the professional city manager and his staff.

Under the non-political council-manager government city employees who faithfully serve the public in turn are protected by the public in their jobs; they don't have to ring doorbells and herd their uncles and their cousins and their aunts to the polls. Municipal service becomes an honored, secure profession like medicine, with new promising possibilities of careers for our boys and girls. Politics has no power to rob them of their human dignity as free souls or to threaten them with loss of their bread and butter.

As years go on, the machine method of choosing our local government will work less and less well. In this election of 1939 the machinery creaked badly in its laborious efforts to choose a ticket.

So let us begin to think about a new and better method.

(Editorial from The Memphis Press-Scimitar, April 2, 1942.)

WAKE UP, MEMPHIS! ACT AS IF YOU WERE FREE— YOU ARE

An entire generation has grown up in Memphis which has never known the practice of democracy—never known what it means to discuss public affairs with complete freedom, never known what it means to evaluate and criticize, with praise and censure, its own government, never known what it means to choose public policies, never known what it means to select and elect its own officials, never known what it means to take civic responsibility.

Now a new generation has gone to war. They are told they are fighting to protect this country from domination by foreign countries. *The Press-Scimitar* believes that would be reason enough to sacrifice and fight for victory, if there were no other. They are also told that they are fighting to preserve democracy and the American way of life, and that is true, for the United States is the freest and most democratic nation on earth. That gives a glory to our cause.

But Memphis does not enjoy the democracy which is found everywhere else in the United States. We have it, but we do not practice it. We accept a local dictatorship instead.

How can we explain this strange phenomenon—a great city giving up democracy which is recognized everywhere as the most precious possession of the Anglo-Saxon world of which it is a part?

Why is there no democracy in Memphis?

The reply formerly was: "Our government is good, our taxes are low, why should we bother?"

But how do the citizens know that their government is good—if it is? They can be sure of that only if they investigate and learn how their government is functioning and meeting its problems. But there is no citizens committe or taxpayers association which is checking up on their government. The only group of citizens which makes any pretense of making recommendations to the government is the bar association—and when the bar association speaks, that's just the machine talking to itself.

We suggest to citizens' groups: Investigate and see for yourself.

If taxes are low, it becomes a question if they are as low as they might be. In these days of war taxes and sacrifice, why should you pay for the political deadwood which is sticking all over your local government?

However, the day has passed when any large number of citizens refrain from activity because they believe that their activity is not needed. They do not think that "everything is all right, why bother." They do not remain inactive because they believe the machine is good, but because they think it's bad. They have such a poor opinion of it, they are so thoroughly convinced of its un-American, undemocratic character, that they fear to exercise their rights and assume their responsibilities of American citizenship. "Why should I stick my neck out?" they say, "the machine would only punish me." Ponder that—fellow citizens!

If that is true, if it is true that this great community is dominated by a group which does not respect the Constitution and laws of the United States which protect every American citizen in the exercise of his rights as a citizen and a voter—then is it not time that a local defense committee be formed to protect the citizens?

Happily, we do not need such a protective committee. The citizens of Memphis are already protected. Memphis is only an island of dictatorship in a sea of democracy. The government at Washington has proved by its actions on many occasions, and most recently by its prosecution and conviction in the federal court at Jonesboro of West Memphis politicians who thought they were "powerful," that it will protect citizens from local oppressors.

The machine has decayed. It is but a shell of its former self. There are not six men in the machine who really desire that it continue—the rest are stooges, who would be relieved if the ever-present fear of being purged were removed from their lives.

Stand alone against the machine, rather than not at all. But is is better that citizens stand together. Think of what ten determined men could do, standing openly and firmly together for the exercise of rights and duties of citizenship which are protected by the great government at Washington. One hundred men could do it easily. In union there is strength.

How long shall the shadow and blight of the Memphis dictatorship be allowed to chill the warm civic life of Memphis?

Shall we wait until its decay has brought material harm to the city, or take steps now, before great damage has been done?

Is there any time when it is not time for American citizens to function as such?

People of Memphis—with all other Americans from Maine to California and from Mississippi to Minnesota—you share the priceless heritage of democracy.

Act as if you were free. YOU ARE.

(Signed editorial from The Memphis Press-Scimitar, January, 1944.)

EDITOR WARNS: 'DON'T HAVE TOO MUCH CONFIDENCE IN THE PRESS-SCIMITAR'

A certain insurance man with offices in the North Memphis Savings Bank Building has on several occasions hinted in his subtle, gentle way that the people of Memphis do not have confidence in *The Press-Scimitar*.

We don't agree with him about that.

The trouble is not that the people of Memphis don't have confidence in this newspaper—they have entirely too much confidence in us.

Consider the situation. There are only two institutions which can be counted on to take a positive stand in the public affairs of this great county of more than 350,000 people. One of them is E.H. Crump and the other is *The Press-Scimitar*.

The Memphis Chamber of Commerce does a nice job of sticking its head in the sand. Perhaps a Chamber of Commerce shouldn't be "in politics." But it should be concerned with business rights and property rights when they are threatened by political power seekers.

The Council of Civic Clubs fails to be "civic"; it never acts in the spirit of independence which American citizenship requires.

The once influential Bar Association has abdicated. The American Legion fights for democracy abroad—but not at home.

The Parent-Teacher Association sits back complacently while political control poisons our educational system and makes a joke of the high-falutin' lectures about character-building, "the American way," etc.

The Association of University Women, composed of the women who have been blessed by the finest in American education, will take a trip to the penal farm and see everything but the penal system which they could do so much to improve.

The luncheon clubs are a little better. Some of them have at last taken a determined stand to keep the machine from picking their presidents. That's only negative, however.

All these organizations, all the citizens in and out of these organizations, know that the only check on the machine is *The Press-Scimitar*. They pay us too great a compliment when they think we are a sufficient check; that their rights will be sufficiently protected by our efforts alone.

We are not going to deny that we do a pretty good job. We're not going to deny that the free press is a very great power. But we are not going to say of your rights, as the machine says to you of your governmental, economic and financial affairs: "Leave everything to us; we'll take care of it."

The free press is only one of the instruments of democracy. Other necessary instruments are organizations of citizens. Unless both function actively, democracy does not function.

Fellow citizens, have confidence in your *Press-Scimitar*. But not too much.

There are before you now two big questions, the answers to which will affect you and your welfare for many years to come. One of them is your city election, the date of which is being juggled about by a boss to suit his personal desires and purposes. The other is the proposed investment of millions of your dollars in a street car system.

You can be sure that Ed Crump and Ed Meeman will say what they please on these questions. But they are only two of Shelby County's many citizens, and should be treated as such. They have only one vote apiece. Remember (and thank God for the boys on Guadalcanal), that you have one, too.

(Guest column in The Birmingham Post, October 21, 1946)

The Crump machine and the leftist revolution are both phases of the same human error—the abdication of individual responsibility, the willingness to accept dictatorship to accomplish some end, the suppression by the individual of his conscience in order that he will find no ojections to what is wrong in the mass movement and may rest, unquestioningly and at ease, as one of the crowd.

Ed Crump started as a reform political leader, and built a machine which became a dictatorship. It must be understood that since this is but an enclave of dictatorship set in a vast, vigorous national democracy, the machine has been severely modified and checked by the surrounding democracy. Crump uses the methods of dictatorship: (1) the assumption that all problems can be left to the all-wisdom of the leader; (2) the one-party system with intolerance of any opposition even in the Democratic primary; (3) the spy system, or at least the propagation of the belief that there is one; (4) the attempt, usually successful, to terrorize into inactivity those who contemplate independent political action.

People may say: "The government must be pretty good or despite dictatorship, people would have risen in revolt long ago." That is exactly what the Memphis government is, "pretty good." It seems to be better than the average local political government, although it has never been subjected to that searching examination that comes with changing administrations. It is not nearly so good as non-political city manager government which many American cities enjoy. (The foundations for what is good in it were laid by a non-machine mayor, Rowlett Paine.)

Crump gives no one a material reason strong enough to stir him to oppose the machine. The average person can get what he wants from the government for the operation of his business or profession. (Even *The Press-Scimitar*, which is independent of Crump, can get adoption of the things the newspaper proposes, more quickly under the dictatorship than would be possible under the slower methods of democracy. For instance, *The Press-Scimitar* put on a campaign to bring TVA power to Memphis. Crump endorsed the project, and it was quickly achieved. The same with an anti-noise campaign which has made Memphis the quietest city in America.)

The reasons for opposing the machine are not so much immediate, practical ones, as long range ones. One must know that short-cuts are costly. The price of dictatorship in Memphis, as in Italy, Germany and Russia, has been high. A whole generation of young people in Memphis have grown to maturity without seeing their parents once take responsibility for democracy or take any part other than a passive one in politics. One can observe, in some individuals, the deterioration of character that comes from being used as a tool by the machine.

The effect of the machine on the state has been bad materially as well as spiritually. State governments sponsored by the machine have been mediocre, and one of them, the scandalous

Luke Lea-Horton administration, left a heritage of debt which the people are still paying.

The Crump machine, outwardly strong, could blow up as suddenly as did its ally, the Cantrell machine, from the revolt of the Athens, Tennessee, GIs.

Some of us who have opposed the Crump machine are more concerned to be certain that it will be succeeded by something better than to speed its passing. We would not want to let loose any of the mob spirit which got into the Athens situation, despite the efforts of the GI leaders to prevent it.

Ten leading citizens of Memphis, simply by banding together for mutual support, at any time could have asserted their right to study and criticize the Memphis government and converted it from a dictatorship to an agency of democracy. It will take only 10 such citizens now to see that the transition is made safely from dictatorship to democracy.

I, for one, would not care to go back to the anarchy of old-fashioned politics, to the screaming babel of a popularity contest between card-passing, baby-kissing candidates. Let us go forward to city manager government which has the advantage of centralized responsibility, but with democratic controls.

(The answer to this, as to every modern problem, is the assumption of responsibility by the individual citizen. He cannot leave everything to the leaders. That is the way to lose everything.)

(Address to the National Conference on Government, sponsored by the National Municipal League, at Boston, November 22, 1948.)

CITIZENS CAN BEAT POLITICIANS AT OWN GAME

There is a crying need for citizen activity in politics to obtain better local government, to obtain national statesmanship which will give citizens a renewed feeling of security in the future of America, to obtain international statesmanship to cope with the threat of Communism and the atom bomb.

Many citizens would like to get into politics and carry elections for the men and measures in which they deeply believe, but they are hindered by the fear that politics is a difficult game which they as amateurs, could not play successfully.

This is a groundless fear, as I will show by telling the story of how a group of American citizens in Memphis, none of whom had any experience in practical politics, extemporized a political organization and defeated a deeply entrenched political machine which was run by shrewd politicians with a long record of continuous success.

What these citizens did in Memphis can be done by other citizens anywhere if they will get together as did these citizens of Memphis.

Tennessee has long been known as the Volunteer State, because of the outstanding record our citizens have made in volunteering their services in this country's wars. Since the elections of 1948, Tennessee deserves to be known as the Volunteer State in another sense—as the state in which citizens volunteered their services in politics not for reasons of personal ambition, or private gain, but because they wanted to achieve the best possible government for their city, their state, their nation, and their world.

What has happened in Tennessee is of the greatest significance. Usually when a political machine has been overthrown after long dominating a community it is because conditions have become intolerable and the people were driven to revolt.

Machines usually fall because business men get tired of carrying a burden of deteriorating service and mounting taxes. It was not so in Memphis. The machine in 1948 was no more intolerable than it had always been. It should always have been intolerable to free men. The only change was that a group of citizens, believing they should do something about world peace, decided that they ought to make an effort to bring about the nomination of the man they believed best fitted to advance the cause of peace in the United States Senate, Estes Kefauver. They did not intend to fight the machine. They intended only to assert their rights to make their own choice for senator. Had the machine let them alone, the machine would probably still be intact. But the machine did not let them alone. Crump lashed out furiously and wildly at Kefauver and his supporters. Under attack, the Kefauver citizens committee became an anti-machine committee, and it became a solid phalanx. It fought back at the machine, fought hard and won. Thus one of the distinctive things about what happened in Memphis is that the anti-machine movement sprang from idealistic, rather than materialistic, motivation.

Another distinctive thing about the Memphis revolt is that it proved that no community has to suffer from a machine.

Machine rule can be ended by a handful of determined men. If a handful of men can end machine rule, as the Memphis experience showed, then a handful of men can also prevent machine rule from ever getting hold in a city. All through the sterile years of machine rule, I had said in editorials and speeches: "If ten substantial citizens will get together and firmly support each other, they can, overnight, end this machine; they can break this spell of fear; they can restore free speech, and free elections to Memphis." When the hour came, it was found that seven men were enough—seven men, firmly standing by each other, broke the grip of tyranny.

So what happened in Memphis is of universal significance; it has lessons for men everywhere who are interested in the vitality of freedom and democracy.

I have said that what has happened in Memphis in 1948 is inspiring and encouraging to other communities. But what happened in Memphis previously should be a warning. For a generation, Memphis had been dominated by a political machine. I have called it a machine. But a more proper designation is a totalitarian dictatorship, modified by the surrounding democracy.

If a dictatorship such as I am about to describe could be set up in a city like Memphis, then it could be set up anywhere in the democratic world. For these was nothing peculiar about Memphis. It has often been said of peoples who succumb to dictatorship in explanation or extenuation of their passivity that they were not of the Anglo-Saxon blood and tradition; that they had had no education in or experience with democracy; or that they were made desperate by economic distress, so as to become indifferent to liberty. None of those things was true in Memphis. Except for its Negro population, Memphis was predominantly Anglo-Saxon; its people were well educated and experienced in democracy. There was nothing wrong with Memphis; if it could happen to Memphis it could happen to any city. Dictatorship sneaked up on Memphis and chained the public mind before people were aware of what was happening to them.

E. H. Crump started as a political leader, became a boss, and then a dictator. He chose all the candidates for the local offices. Not only that, he decided what candidates for United States senator, governor, and even president, Memphians should support. A candidate given an overwhelming vote at one election would get a handful of ballots at the next election if the machine, for its own reasons, fell out with him. The biggest men in the machine were made to learn who was boss. Even the powerful Senator McKellar was humiliated; in one election he was not allowed to carry his own precinct for his personal choice of governor.

At first the machine kept hands off the schools and the courts. But finally they were taken over. Young leaders who showed independence were given jobs. Citizens organizations were infiltrated and taken over by the same methods which Communists were later to use. Neighborhood civic clubs, originally planned to represent the people in their relations with the city and county governments, by the strategic activities of city employees were made instead to represent the city administration in its program of controlling public opinion.

In the bar association, votes of lawyers who were on the public payroll—local, state and federal—were used by the machine to get control of the organization, and for years the machine dictated all decisions of the bar association.

Fear to oppose the machine, or even to dissent from it, became widespread.

How great was that fear I will illustrate by these incidents.

The city administration proposed a large bond issue. There was no public discussion of the merits of the various proposals, except by our newspaper, *The Press-Scimitar*. We analyzed them, recommended approval of certain of them, rejection of others. It seemed to us that other citizens should express their opinions of the proposals as we did.

After a Rotary meeting I happened to see two friends of mine, men of large fortune, standing together talking. I walked up to them. I said:

"You men have a large stake in this community as taxpayers. The city administration has submitted a bond issue with a lot of proposals. Why don't you get up a citizens committee to make recommendations as to what should be approved and what should not?"

One of the men gasped and said: "You don't know what you are asking!"

The other said nothing.

People feared that their taxes would be raised, that they would be arrested, that they would be beat up. Actually, the machine seldom made reprisals against dissenters. There were just enough reprisals to give some ground for the universal fear.

Like all dictatorships, the machine did not rely on terror alone. They relied perhaps even more on propaganda. The propaganda was that the government was so good that there was no reason why a citizen should take any interest in it, except to vote for its continuance without question. People said:

"We're not being hurt, so why stick your neck out?"

To experts in government, the local government, while better than many cities have, would seem far below what has been achieved where citizens take an active interest in government.

If the local government had been as good as the machine represented, it would still not have justified the robbing of the people of Memphis of their right to choose governors, senators, and presidents, because the machine chose some very poor material for them.

With 60,000 managed votes in Memphis and Shelby County, the machine was able to dictate state nominations. Not often were good men willing to run. They weren't willing to make a deal with the machine, and they didn't think they could win without it.

But in 1948 Representative Estes Kefauver, who had made a brilliant record as representative from the Chattanooga district in the House, aspired to the Senate, and was willing to give up a sure thing in his home district for a chance in the larger field. I advised him, as I did every prospective independent candidate for state office, that the thing to do was to make a direct appeal to the people of Memphis and Shelby County for their support, by-passing the machine, and treating the people as if they were free—as of course they were; they needed only to act that way. That was his idea too.

One day I was talking over the phone to J. Charles Poe. He had been state conservation commissioner. Sam Nickey, Jr., enlightened young president of Nickey Brothers Lumber Company, was a member of the conservation commission, and he had been so impressed with Mr. Poe that he induced him to come to Memphis and join his company as an official.

"I am going to come out for Estes Kefauver," Poe said, in a matter of fact way. "I knew him when I lived in Chattanooga and this talk by some of his opponents that he is a dangerous radical just makes me laugh."

I tried to conceal my surprise. People in Memphis didn't "come out" for candidates. Only one man "came out" and everybody else said "me too."

Kefauver came to Memphis. Charlie and I invited about 100 people to come to his hotel suite to meet him. Forty came; that was a good percentage under the circumstances prevailing at that time. For on one of Kefauver's early visits, our paper could not find anyone bold enough to consent to be photographed with him.

In that first meeting were four men who became the nucleus of the Kefauver committee.

There was Poe.

There was Dr. Henry Gotten, who had just done an outstanding civic service. I had been a dinner guest in his home one evening. We were talking about the Baptist Hospital, and how unsatisfactory conditions there were. He said he had made a report about it to the Medical Society.

"Would you give out that report for publication?" I asked.

"Yes," he said. It was a startling answer, as startling and as welcome as Charlie Poe's calm announcement of his support of Kefauver was later to be.

Dr. Gotten and other doctors, working with Baptist laymen and *The Press-Scimitar*, cleaned up the bad conditions at Baptist Hospital, and it is now a splendid institution. Like the city's politics, this institution had suffered from one-man rule, the rule not of Crump but of its long-time manager, and the unwillingness of the public and the medical profession to touch sacred cows. The clean-up was proof to me of a statement I had often made:

"Citizens working alone can accomplish much. A newspaper working alone can accomplish much. But citizens and a newspaper working together can accomplish anything."

So Dr. Gotten in an interview the next day came out for Kefauver and became Committeeman No. 2.

Also in that meeting with Kefauver was W.M. Barr, paint-remover manufacturer. Bill Barr had just come back from war. It didn't even occur to Bill to hesitate. "It doesn't make sense to me," he said, "to risk your life for democracy in foreign countries and then do nothing about it at home."

The fourth man was Edwin A. Dalstrom, conservative paper company executive. He wanted to come out for Kefauver, but he had to be satisfied that Kefauver's vote against the Taft-Hartley bill did not mean that he would blindly vote for its repeal. Kefauver later satisfied him and many other business men that he regarded the Taft-Hartley law as the law of the land, entitled to fair trial on its merits, and that he would not support any amendments unless actual experience under the law had shown that amendments were needed.

The interest of Lucius E. Burch, Jr. was enlisted. Here is a man to watch; we have seen only the beginning of him. He is a scion of some of the South's leading families. There are stories of his athletic youth; how he showed his wealthy parents that he could earn his own living, hunting and trapping in Alaska; how he entered a tavern in evening clothes, a fact resented physically by some toughs already present, who unfortunately learned, to their dismay, that underneath the evening clothes was the powerful frame of an intercollegiate boxing champion. He learned philosophy while studying at Vanderbilt in his native Nashville. He was influenced by the Fugitive Group there; men who interpreted the South as standing for something better than the finance capitalism of the North, namely agrarianism and distribution. One of that Group, Donald Davidson, wrote a poem, "Tall Men." Burch is one of those tall men, tall not only physically, but mentally and spiritually. He came to Memphis to join his uncle's law firm. At his uncle's death Lucius became the head of it. Burch coolly surveyed the Memphis scene. He saw the boss browbeating everybody. He was not prepared to open a fight on the machine. But he would not be browbeaten; he would go his way, and do what he pleased as if the machine did not exist. That he did. The machine watched with some apprehension this man who could not be terrorized.

Some years ago Burch read Clarence Streit's "Union Now." He became convinced that federation of the democracies was the answer. He sent the book to Edmund Orgill, head of Orgill Bros. & Company, wholesale hardware dealers, a business which has been in the Orgill family since it was founded a hundred years ago (1847). He sent it to Edmund while Edmund was on vacation and it got a thorough reading—an example of the careful timing which always characterizes Lucius. Edmund became convinced, and a more earnest advocate, even, than Lucius himself. Edmund formed a Memphis chapter of Federal Union, Inc., made speeches before many organizations, and a strong sentiment was established in our community for the Streit solution. Now what has this to do with local government? Plenty. If men were committed to such a great object, that they thought of it, worked for it, day and night, they could not escape a feeling of compulsion to use their efforts to elect someone who would carry it out. Our incumbent senator, Tom Stewart, whose term was expiring, had been dropped by the machine to which he had been slavishly loyal, because they had cold-bloodedly decided he couldn't win. But he refused to be dropped and was running on his own. Stewart was an isolationist, and Burch and Orgill could find no hope in him. But Kefauver had made a record in the House of intelligent support of measures of international co-operation.

Would Kefauver go all the way and support the idea of Federal Union? Conferences were held. The idea was not foreign to Kefauver's thought; in fact he believed in it, and declared himself for it.

Burch had committed himself to Kefauver in the hope that he would stand for Federal Union; Orgill committed himself on the assurance of it.

If they were working for democracy on a transatlantic scale, how could they fail to assume their responsibilities at home?

They could not do otherwise. If personal freedom was so indispensable that it was to be made the sine qua non of international organization, how could the advocates of Federal Union allow a political machine which insulted human dignity to bar their path?

So Burch and Orgill, two men of great weight and gifts of leadership, were added to the committee. And there were six.

The Citizens Committee for Kefauver was in the making, but it had not been announced. Word of what was going on surely reached the ears of the boss. The machine's spy system wasn't nearly as good as the machine liked people to think it was, but it would have had to be very poor indeed if it had not informed the boss of what was going on. The boss put a page ad in the papers which screamed that Kefauver was a dangerous Red. Those who had studied the methods of the boss interpreted this as not so much a direct effort to defeat Kefauver as an indirect effort to serve notice on these citizens what kind of a campaign they were in for if they should dare to come out openly in independent political activity.

Perhaps the faces of some members of the committee blanched as they read the boss' tirade. The boss had a gift for invective which he did not hesitate to use. Fear of personal attack had been a greater deterrent than fear of arrest or increased taxes in dissuading citizens from assuming their responsibilities as citizens.

The citizens faced this danger and decided they could stand it. If they were never, in the weeks to come, to open a paper without wondering what advertisement might be in it directed

toward them; if they were never to tune in on a political broadcast without knowing some stooge of the machine would be
taking their name in ridicule or smear—well, they could stand
it. Democracy was worth that price.

So the committee announced itself.

The announcement was a sensation. If was the first time in a
generation that citizens, purely as citizens, without connection
with a political movement, had taken a stand for what they
believed.

The name of Orgill, in that statement, was itself a sensation. For there is no name in Memphis of higher repute than
that of Orgill. For a hundred years it had stood for vigorous
business enterprise, for fair dealing with customers and
employes, for generous humanitarian activities, for decent personal conduct. Edmund Orgill, the head of the business, had
also been president of the Chamber of Commerce, the Rotary
Club, and the Community Chest.

Having made the plunge, the committee lost no time getting into action. Headquarters were opened in Hotel Peabody.

Kefauver was brought to Memphis for a luncheon. Five
hundred people dared to come—and didn't think they had done
anything daring. They didn't step out of range when the news
cameras caught them with Kefauver. Crump had called
Kefauver a pet coon, implying that he was tricky and you had
better watch what he would do when you weren't looking.
Kefauver rejoined, "I'M NOT MR. CRUMP'S pet coon," put on
a coonskin cap, Tennessee pioneer style, grinned happily, and
the campaign was on its way toward its astounding victory over
John R. Mitchell, a Middle Tennessee judge, the machine
candidate, and Stewart, the former machine senator.

I said there were seven. Who was the seventh? To the
luncheon came O.D. Bratton. As a lumberman, he had had
dealings with the affable Chattanooga congressman, found him
energetic and fair, liked him, and wanted to see him in the
Senate. It was as simple as that. It just didn't occur to him that
he should consider whether the machine objected to his making
his choice. So O.D. Bratton was added to the committee. His
matter-of-factness, his sense of humor, made him invaluable.

Not one of these seven men had had any previous political
experience. Yet they proceeded to set up a political organization
without difficulty. The same intelligence, shrewd perception of
character, and organizing ability which had won them success in
their business and professions, and in their civic work, was all

that was needed in the political work they were now undertaking. And the fact that they were working not to get jobs for themselves, or favors, or personal power or prestige, but for a cause that was bigger than themselves, gave them an inspiration which professional politicians could not have. The professional politician runs an awful bluff on the citizen. He makes the citizen think that politics is something mysterious, difficult, which must be left to the professional.

Well, these amateurs called the bluff. They organized wards, and held resounding rallies. They card-indexed supporters, workers and voters. They got people to serve as election officials and watchers.

And the women! What a job they did. Jennie Burford Gardner, who, as literary editor of the Commercial Appeal, had been quietly but firmly independent of the machine, could not serve herself, but got her sister, Mrs. Robert Marshall, to serve. Mrs. Henry L. Rau, Jr. served. The third woman chairman was Mrs. Lawrence Coe.

All sorts of talent, hidden thru the years, flocked to the citizens committee to help.

Young lawyers—Homer Armstrong, Bill McTighe, Ham Patterson, Bailey Brown, Jim Manire, and many others were in to help with the organization work and to make street corner and ward speeches. Sometimes the Citizens Committee had as many as 30 speakers out over the city in one night.

A young advertising man—M.J. Vosse—came in and said he wanted to help. When Edmund Orgill heard he was in the advertising business, he immediately enlisted him to draw up ads. "But I've never done a political advertisement," said Vosse. "Go ahead and try," said Orgill. "O.K., I'll give you the ads I know about," answered Vosse.

The results were astounding to the politicians—such things as a quarter-page ad on the woman's page, directed to women, saying: "Biggest Bargain in Town—Poll Tax only $2—and it gives you the privilege of voting for Estes Kefauver, a great statesman, for the United States Senate."

It's funny, as the humorist said, how many things people believe that "ain't so". One such belief is that women talk too much. No one talked less than the women, and I am thinking especially of Mrs. Coe. In fact, you had to beg her for an expression of opinion. But no one contributed sounder judgment; no one worked harder in the task of organizing the wards.

The work of the women, who said little and did much, is beyond praise.

Labor unions made a magnificent contribution. The labor unions have really convinced their members that every American should register, pay his poll tax where required, work in his ward, and vote. What a democracy we would have if every other organization in America would as successfully convince their members to assume responsibility!

The greatest praise must be given to those citizens— business men, professional men, union members, women— who faced up to the machine at the firing line of this battle, the polling places, as officials, watchers and workers.

There is much talk about clean, fair elections. We talked about better laws in Tennessee and since our victory we have got them. We talked about getting the FBI to watch the election in Memphis and that would have been a fine thing. But there is only one way to get and keep clean elections. Whether laws be poor or good, enforcement good or bad, the citizens who want clean elections have got to go down in the polling places and see that the votes are fairly cast and fairly counted. That's what the brave citizens of Memphis did. The primary was fairer than any primary had been in years, and to our amazement, as we heard the returns come in that night, we actually carried 27 precincts for Kefauver and made a good showing everywhere.

In the final election, unfairness was held to a minimum and the independent candidates, who had become the official Democratic candidates, Kefauver for senator and Gordon Browning for governor, carried the county handsomely. By this time the citizen amateurs had become the official Democratic party.

Let me give you a few examples of election frauds and how they have been cleaned up.

I will read the full text of the transcript of a telephone conversation obtained in Memphis at the time of the August 5 primary and presented to the Tennessee Election Law Revision Commission by Lucius Burch, member of the Shelby County Citizens Committee. The conversation was between a special investigator and a Shelby County precinct official. The precinct official thought he was talking to someone on his side and told how he intended to steal the election. Mr. Burch submitted the transcript to the commission to show the need for voting machines. Fictitious names have been substituted in the transcript:

Q. Hello, has Mr. Roe come in yet?

A. Yes, he's here, just a minute.

Q. Hello.

Q. Mr. Doe, again.

A. Mr. Doe? All right.

Q. We know you have been taking care of things out there for a long time. Has Coe gotten there yet?

A. Sir?

Q. Has Coe gotten there yet?

A. Coe? Yes. He went to the city.

Q. Has he reached your house yet?

A. No, he isn't here yet.

Q. Well now, we know you have been handling it for a long time, but we want to know just how you and Smith are going to take care of this thing as we feel there's going to be a lot of Kefauver people out there.

A. Well, listen, we are going to take care of it the very best way we can. We don't know just what's going to happen out here yet, we don't know how many watchers we're going to have. Of course, I know there is one woman that is looking after Kefauver's interest and that's Mrs. Brown. Now if I can get a chance I think I can handle her pretty nicely.

Q. Well now, just how do you all plan to handle her and what do you all plan to do to keep those Kefauver votes out?

A. I would like to handle her with some liquor if I could get her to drink it. If I can, I can make it go over big.

Q. Well now, what about those Negroes that are going to vote for Kefauver down there?

A. Those Negroes?

Q. Yes sir.

A. By golly, we'll have to cut every one of those out we possibly can.

Q. How are you going to cut them out, Roe?

A. Well, a lot of them are so darn ignorant they can't write their name and, of course, that gets them.

Q. Uh Huh.

A. That's one way to get them, and the other way to get them is to, uh, well, you don't have to let every vote go and sometimes you can't help it, but sometimes you can switch votes around and we try to block everything we possibly can, that's all we can do. Until we get into the fight we don't know what's going to happen.

Q. You are going to take care of it now?

A. I'm going to do my best, and I think Mrs. Smith will, too.

Q. Well, what did she tell you to do?

A. Well, I haven't had a serious talk with Mrs. Smith. I'm going to have one with her tonight.

Q. Didn't she tell you what Blank said?

A. No, I haven't seen her for two days. You see I'm working over her at Blank liquor store.

Q. Who has been your contact man?

A. My contact man? All the contact I've had with anybody is Mrs. Smith.

Q. She hasn't told you anything about how she wanted you to do?

A. No she hasn't yet.

Q. Well, you have been handling it in the past together.

A. We have, that's right.

Q. Well, have you been able to get rid of them before?

A. Well, you can ask her how I handled it the last Browning election. She'll tell you that I handled it pretty nicely and we had watchers at that time.

Q. We want you to do it the way you want to do it but we want to be sure that you do it right.

A. You know I'm not so well qualified perhaps in some things along that line and I'm willing to take advice and any suggestions that's been made to her, well, I guess that she will tell me about them and we'll try to carry them out. We know one thing, we have got to do it in a way we don't want our box throwed out, we don't want to have any trouble with anybody.

Q. We don't want any rough stuff out there.

A. No, we don't want anything like that, and we're not going to have anything like that because I have always handled them. They are mostly Negroes you know and I don't have but very few white people and I have never had any trouble. Now I always try to . . . in the last election, I'll tell you what I done in Browning's election when Browning run. When I come to the polls that morning and fixing up the polling place in comes a couple of gentlemen and told me they was watching for Mr. Browning. I says, all right gentlemen, very good, I'm very glad to have you with us and I'm going to show you just what I want you to do and what you've got to do. And I took one of them off and I said, now I think I can talk to you, young man. I said, you are out here to make a piece of money, and I just don't think that you give a durn which way this vote's going anyway. You are working for a day's work and I'm going to tell you one thing, we are going to beat you here today but I don't think you are going to collect a durn dime today, which happened. Now it really happened. Now you work on your brother there and if he wants to talk just tell him to come to me. Well, directly the young fellow came to me and I told him, I said, now you fellows just keep your mouth shut, I'm for Browning, too. Now just keep your mouth shut and don't take me for what I say but just keep your mouth shut and watch me, I'm going to show you I'm going to have a fair election. They said, all right. So they did and they never opened their chops. When it come to counting the votes I told them "you fellows stand over at the far side of the room now," and I took the ballot box and went over on the far side of the room and kept my back to the wall and I commenced calling the ballots and that is all there was to it. So I think I can handle this the same way.

Q. Well, all right.

A.   That was my plan then. Now if there is anything different from that now why maybe I'll change it a little bit.

Q. I'll call you in thirty minutes.

A. All right.

Q. Thank you.

There was Gummer's store. Seven years ago the machine recorded a vote of 549 for the machine candidate for governor to only one for the opposition. A *Press-Scimitar* reporter, Carl Marsh, publicly claimed that one vote as the one that he had cast. That started things. Another citizen stepped forward and said that he also had voted for the opposition candidate. One after another followed until there were nine. Only three votes had been recorded for the opposition candidate for United States senator; but nine persons said they had voted for him. Many others have since said they voted independently but did not care to say so publicly for fear of machine reprisals. Here was conclusive proof of the machine's fraudulent methods; and the machine has never attempted to refute it. In this election of November 2, that same reporter was present at the same polling place all day and was able to report that the election was entirely fair. Thus, citizens have wrought a change.

And there was Stewartville. The Memphis-Shelby machine's power was built originally by the practice of hauling truckloads of Negroes to the polls and voting them, often more than once. Thus an immense vote was built up with which to overwhelm the votes of free voters in Memphis and elsewhere in the state. At no box was this practiced on a larger scale than Stewartville. Negroes were hauled to Stewartville in school buses by the hundreds, sometimes from adjoining counties.

Let me tell you what happened at Stewartville in 1948. In the primary, without dependable watchers, the machine carried Stewartville by a 1000 to 77 majority, or approximately that. In the general election, Bill McTighe and Dolph Clark went out. Bill dressed for the occasion wearing his GI combat boots. But the machine gave them practically no trouble all day, although it tried to vote Negroes in truckloads, as we showed pictorially. Then—the scene which really showed that times had changed occurred late that night, 1 or 2 a.m. Bill McTighe and Dolph Clark came straggling into the election commission office carrying the Stewartville box, Bill still in his combat boots. The machine gave up and had them bring it to town.

The count showed that the machine workers out there had thrown Stewartville to the Republicans—Roy Acuff, the hill-billy singer, was given 368 and Browning 277. But we could stand it. For Shelby County as a whole, and the state as a whole, went overwhelmingly for Browning.

Thus the revolution against bossism which began in 1946 with a GI revolt against a branch of the Crump machine at Athens, Tennessee, came to a triumphant conclusion with a GI incident in the citadel of the machine, Shelby County.

What is the significance of what happened in Memphis?

First, Kefauver could not have been elected without it. Kefauver, unsupported by an old-line political organization, had done a magnificent job of going over the state and lining up votes for himself on a personal basis. But the loose organization which he had over the state could hardly have swung it for him if the workers had not been encouraged by seeing a fight being made in the home city of the state machine, not only to hold down the usual inflated majority for the machine candidate but actually to get a sizeable bloc of votes counted for Kefauver. His manager had said before it was done, "the setting up of an organization in Memphis would mean a difference of 50,000 votes in our favor in the state as a whole."

The victory means that the dictatorship which has so long dominated Tennessee is a thing of the past. Statesmen can now run for office without having to deal with a machine or face the handicap of a large bloc of controlled votes against them. The last statesman to defeat the rising power of the machine had been Cordell Hull; we look upon Estes Kefauver as the beginning of a new line.

There was another statesman elected on November 5, 1948. Gordon Browning who gave us a capable, enlightened administration of the governor's office in 1936 to 1938, was returned to that job for a second term. Supporting him valiantly in that campaign, was Representative Albert Gore, Fourth District congressman, another statesman, and a fine, brave committee in Shelby County composed of Robert L. Taylor, Gilmer Richardson, Henry Buck, Rembert Moon, and L.W. Booth, head of the veterans committee.

And what of the future in Memphis and Shelby County?

The air of Memphis is clean again.

Not from smoke, or fog (for we are a river town), but from a choking fear that has been so strong for an entire generation that it actually stifled something more important than a man's nostrils—his freedom of expression with his neighbors and associates.

That is all gone now. It left suddenly—almost like a flash of lightning on the morning of August 6, 1948, when the people of Memphis awoke and found that the Crump machine had been smashed by their votes. Crump remained an influential political leader, but he was no longer a dictator.

To hear merchants in a community, standing out in front of their stores, talking politics freely and discussing community and city affairs and taxes would not be unusual in almost any part of America. But it was so unusual in Memphis on the morning of August 6—the day after the primary—that people began to talk about this new freedom which had always been assured them under our Constitution and laws. And this freedom of thought and expression is here to stay.

Will the Memphis citizens who defeated the politicians quit? Will they go back to their businesses and professions, as many feared they would, and let the old politicians come back to a position where they can again deny citizens their rights and liberties? Or let some new bunch of politicians do the same thing?

They will not. The day after election they made it clear that they would not let the people down. They issued a statement they would work for permanent registration, civil service for city employees, a "Little Hatch Act" to keep them from being regimented for political service against their will and against the people, and eventual council-manager government.

We Memphians never do things by halves. We have been pronounced at one time the safest city in the country, the cleanest city, the healthiest city, and city freest from fire, the city with the least noise. We have been known as the city with the most tyrannical political machine.

There's just one thing left for us to be the best of. Now it is not considered, since the 1948 national election, wise for a newspaperman to make a prediction. But I am going to make one. I am going to predict that Memphis will have the best non-political council-manager government in the nation. I predict we will have the most active citizens' movement, city officials who are appointed on the strictest merit system and most brilliantly qualified, city employees who are most secure from political exploitation, and the finest all-round governmental performance of any city in the country.

VII

The Memphis Years, Continued: Touring Tenant Farms in Arkansas With Guy Tugwell and Henry Wallace—Plan for a Model Farm Community

My paper defended the white people who fell afoul of the Crump organization. We championed the Negroes who were arrested without right, beaten up by police and denied legal rights. Similarly, we defended the tenant farmers in counties outside of Memphis, when their efforts to organize were met with violence. Violence was insupportable, but that does not mean that a tenant farmers' union is viable.

We supported the efforts of the Franklin D. Roosevelt administration to improve the condition of the tenant farmers, including the experiments in model farm communities by Rex Tugwell and his Resettlement Administration. While these experiments were never perfected, there was so much good in them that it is a shame that they were completely liquidated. In particular the design and beauty of the community near Pine Bluff, Ark. lifted my heart as I saw it on a tour with Tugwell and his chief, Henry Wallace, whom Tugwell was trying to sell, without complete success, on what he was doing.

At that time I offered a plan for a farm community which I still think offers the permanent security of private ownership and keeps the door always open for experiments in the economic advantages and the spiritual fellowship of the co-operative, the sturdy human joy of the individual home and family, the divine joy of community fellowship, and, if the presence of God is practiced, the fellowship of the kingdom of heaven itself.

(*Editorial, in the form of an open letter, from The Memphis Press-Scimitar, September, 1936.*)

To Governor Futrell's Commission on the Sharecropper Problem—

Gentlemen:

This newspaper would like to lay before you our ideas on the problem you will discuss at Hot Springs Monday, September 21.

We believe that only a little can be accomplished by attempting to improve the lot of the sharecroppers under the present land and agricultural economy. Our object should be to replace the present economy, gradually, square mile by square mile, with a new and sound one of independent farmers in which the sharecropper will have no place.

The present economy will not work much longer, not merely because critics and investigators have pointed out that the lot of the sharecropper is unhappy, but because there is a profound change under way in the market.

It will be safest if we assume that foreign production of cotton will steadily increase. This production has been stimulated by two causes: America's high tariff, which has made it difficult for foreign countries to sell us enough of their own products to enable them to pay for our cotton, and their own economic nationalism, which causes them to desire to be independent of us. We hope that these causes will be largely removed.

But even if they are, it would be foolish to expect that foreign production of cotton will not increase. Other countries have lands suitable for cotton production; they have enterprise—why should they not develop this new crop? We had better make our plans on the expectation that they will.

Liberal internal policies in the United States such as those of Franklin D. Roosevelt will increase the purchasing power of Americans and enable them to buy some of the cotton we now send abroad. But since we now send 60 per cent of our crop abroad, the domestic increase is not likely to make up for foreign losses.

We need diversification, not in the old sense merely of raising food and feed crops, but in a new sense. We need to have communities of independent, intelligent land-owning farmers who can not only raise their own subsistence, but change their crops with changing markets.

That great changes are ahead is apparent. Just what those changes will be we do not know. Can we find a farm system which is likely to work whatever form these changes take? We think so.

Let us lay out, in our mind's eye, the farm community that ought to be.

Let us take a great circle of land. It need not be an exact circle, of course; a square or an irregularly shaped tract, not too narrow, would do as well. We say circle because that suggests the idea. Divide this into pieces as you would a pie, except that you reserve a tract at the heart for common purposes, such as forest, pasture and the like. Each of these "slices" represents the homestead of a farm family. His house lies somewhere toward the center of the tract. Near it are his garden, his small crops, his chickens, his hogs, or whatever little side crop he might care to raise.

The outer portion of his land would be clear of buildings. Here he would raise his major crop. Thus the major crop land of all the small farmers would lie together. This would permit the efficient co-operative use of all existing labor-saving machinery such as an airplane cotton duster, and any that the future may bring.

The success of such a farm community would not be dependent on the success of co-operation. If co-operation failed, the farmers would still have their land to farm without co-operation. But such a layout would induce co-operation, and such co-operation would raise the level of our farmer's lives. Such a layout would permit them to build an independent, enduring family life rooted in the soil. At the same time they would not be at a disadvantage in competing with the great plantation which would lie next door to them or with the great cotton ranches of the Argentine and Brazil. Such a layout would permit them to change their major crop, if economic conditions demanded, from cotton to corn, or soy beans, or whatever plant industry and the home consumer in any particular year demanded. It would permit the individual farmers to abandon any common major crop, and each choose a different crop of his own, if such extreme diversification seemed advantageous.

The government ought to start encouraging the establishment of such communities. Let a government agency buy such large tracts of land, divide it into slices, and lease the slices on indefinite leases to good farmers.

We say "lease" rather than "sell" because under a lease terms can be laid down which will prevent a return of the evils we are trying to cure. These terms can make it impossible for the farmer to mortgage his holdings. The right to mortgage is not the right to possess land; it is only the right to lose it. Let the lease provide also that if the lessor wishes to give up farming, the lease may be transferred only to some other good farmer. The lease can also be used to prevent soil waste.

Let this opportunity at land ownership—for it is nonetheless true ownership even though wisely conditioned—go only to ambitious men. Let it go to the cream of the present sharecroppers—those who need only an opportunity to make good. It would be a waste of time to give this opportunity to any shiftless family, for they would be foredoomed to failure before they started. Let the opportunity be open to good farmers from anywhere, for instance from the drouth sections of the Middle West.

While this opportunity should be open to good Negro farmers, it should be recognized that the South needs more white farm owners, and a studied effort should be made to increase the proportion of white men on the soil. This need will be more apparent as we get away from a cotton economy.

Let us not think in terms of huge federal appropriations. If a lot of money is spent quickly, it will be spent unwisely, and the program will fall into disrepute and be abandoned before our problem has been solved. We must make a start, acquire experience, and as the government agency learns to do this job of assisting a group of farmers to establish a community, let it have more money to spend.

Why should not this agency be the Resettlement Administration? The RA has been working somewhat along these lines. It has, of course, made some mistakes, but it has also acquired a fund of valuable experience, so that it will make fewer mistakes in the future than a new agency would make.

In particular, T. Roy Reid, the director of the Resettlement Administration for Arkansas, Mississippi and Louisiana, has shown himself to be a practical man. His experience should be called upon in the solution of this problem.

The sharecropper system is the worst possible system. But the worst often turns to the best. If, resolutely and hopefully, we work out a constructive handling of this problem, we can build the most wholesome rural life and the soundest rural prosperity that is to be found anywhere on the globe.

In this task you will have the earnest co-operation of this newspaper.

What's wrong with this? Nothing that I can see. It is an example of "not either, or" but "both, and". Yet I got no attention for it. It is not true that a good idea necessarily makes its way to adoption because of its intrinsic merit—many good ideas, long ago offered, have not yet been adopted. But now I am trying again with this one. Do something about this, somebody!

VIII

Visit to Nazi Germany: Impressions of Hitler—Bloody Songs at a Youth Meeting—Hitlerism Born in Paris, London, Prague, Warsaw and Washington—Injustices Toward German People

I visited Germany as Hitler was taking over and talked with both Hitler and his German victims.

(From The Memphis Press-Scimitar, August 7, 1933.)

The Hitler party came to a dominant position in Germany by the use of propaganda, most of which was unscrupulous and some of which was false. It seized absolute power by force and ruthlessly stamped out all opposition.

But today, while an unconverted minority of the German people scarcely dares privately to express its doubts, much less publicly to express its grievances, the Hitler party seems to have the enthusiastic support of the majority.

The Hitler red flag with the white swastika flies in all public places and in countless homes. The German national flag is seldom flown without the Hitler flag alongside of it, but the Hitler flag often flies alone. Some go so far as to fly the German flag with the swastika super-imposed on it. Hitler pictures and postcards are everywhere. Every city has a street named for Adolph Hitler.

A CROWD PERSONALITY

Hitler has a crowd personality. Such a crowd personality can sense the mood of a mass of men, can interpret and voice the yearnings which have been unexpressed and perhaps even not fully known to themselves. Such a man may have the "will to power." As he instinctively voices the mood of the crowd, so also

he instinctively strives to dominate it. And the crowd yields to
its hero and wishes to be dominated by him. Hitler does not
partake of alcohol, but he is drinking what is said to be the most
intoxicating draught in the world—the sway of the minds and
hearts of millions of people.

Hitler at another time and place might have been a religious leader. The fervor he inspires is religious in character. It is a
matter of the emotions rather than the reason.

BECOMES NATIONAL SAINT

Already Hitler has been elevated to the position of a national saint, and he is "worshipped" as such much in the same
way as Lenin is worshipped by the Russian Communists.

The yearning of the German crowd to which Hitler ap-
pealed was the yearning for prosperity and for equality with
other nations. . . .

That it takes form from Hitler is due to his amazing appeal
to the crowd. "What an orator!", said a young liberal, who had
been converted almost against his will.

The Germans still tell you of the vast meeting in the
Templehof airport in Berlin on May 1, the International Labor
Day which Hitler stole from the Communists as he did a great
deal of Communist technique. Here Hitler addressed a million
and a half people. The Germans still boast of the remarkable
discipline of that crowd. For there was not a single accident,
though seven babies were born in the crowd.

Probably they were all named Adolph Hitler, girls as well
as boys. What kind of a country will those seven babies grow up
in?

(From The Memphis Press-Scimitar, August 8, 1933.)

Germany today is imbued with war-time psychology.

The country seethes with militant patriotism.

The emotion is directed at Communism, which is painted
by the National Socialists as a force which threatened to seize
supreme power had they not done so, against Germans who are
pacifists or international in their viewpoint, against the wrongs
done to Germany by the Treaty of Versailles. It voices rever-
ence for Germany's past, especially that which is militaristic in
it, and confidence in her own inner strength to solve her problems with or without the help of the rest of the world.

War-time psychology in any country is a mob psychology,

unreasoning and intolerant of any opposition, or even any lack of faith in the crowd's objectives. Jews, because they are called non-German and internationalist in sympathy, have been driven from public life and boycotted in private business, though physical outrages were probably confined to the few acts of extremists in the first days of the Nazi revolution.

BROOK NO INTERFERENCE

All parties except the Hitler party, including the moderate Social Democratic party which was the largest party in Germany prior to the Hitler regime, have been suppressed. Leaders of the opposition who have not fled to foreign lands have been sent to concentration camps—euphemistically called "educational camps" because an effort is made to convert them to the Hitler nationalism.

I walked along the streets of a large German city with a German liberal, not a Socialist. He pointed out a large recreation park.

"This was bought and paid for by the Socialists with their money. It has been confiscated and turned over to the National Socialists. What an outrage!

HELD BY FEAR OF JAIL

"If I were overheard talking this way, I would be sent to jail."

In a hotel lobby a leading German business man, a former liberal, looked around to see of anyone was listening before he dared to voice his perplexity at the new conditions.

One German editor on whom I called let me do all the talking on the question of the new regime. Apparently he was not going to run the risk of getting into trouble by being quoted in America, though I had no intention of quoting anyone.

Another newspaper editor spoke favorably of the new regime.

"It must be difficult for you foreigners to understand the new Germany as it was difficult for us older people to adjust ourselves at first to the new day."

CONVERSION SEEMS FORCED

It seemed to me a forced self-conversion on his part. It reminded me of the American liberals, who, caught in the tide of mass emotion during the World War, came to believe that it

was a "war to end war" and that Germany's defeat would result
in a "new day" in which "democracy" would be "saved." But
they woke up to find that Germany's defeat had not brought a
new day, but a terrible aftermath, in which there was less
democracy than before. German intellectuals who have convinced themselves that there is a "new day" will probably wake
up to find that the world has not changed. They will find that
national passions and racial hatreds are not the foundation on
which to build a brighter world.

This brow-beating of the mature and the old is one of the
tragedies of the nationalistic movement in Germany. In the
post-war period one sympathized with the youth who had been
cheated of that youth by the war. Today in Germany it is the
mature and the old who are being robbed by ruthless youth of
what they have won by a lifetime of effort.

Old and experienced men have been forced out of jobs
because the wisdom born of experience would not permit them
to embrace the extremes of the National Socialist movement.

Said one such man, threatened with dismissal from a prominent position:

"The Nationalist Socialists are making terrible mistakes in
their recklessness. But it only makes us sad to see it. For after
all, they are our boys."

(From The Memphis Press-Scimitar, August 9, 1933.)

Hitler and his National Socialists are firmly in the saddle in
Germany.

With all opposition parties disbanded, the property of the
more militant of them confiscated, and their leaders interned in
concentration camps or in refuge abroad, there is no place for
revolt to start.

Nor is Hitler's strength merely negative. To a traveler it
appears that he has the majority of people behind him, enthusiastically supporting him and believing that he will bring
regeneration and prosperity to their country.

Copying the Russian Communist methods of governing as
he copied their methods of propaganda, Hitler is trying to make
over Germany into a wholly nationalist state as Lenin set about
making Russia into a wholly communist state. This means alter-
ing people as well as institutions.

PARTIES ARE OUT

Instead of a horizontal division of the people into parties, Hitler proposes only a vertical division of people into associations of various industrial, professional, and amateur groups all united in a burning love for the Fatherland.

Perhaps the most significant phase of the program is the molding of children into intense patriots. The Boy and Girl Scout organizations are not permitted, because they stress international brotherhood. Children can belong only to the organization of Hitler youth.

Even Hitler's death would not arrest the program, for Hermann Goering, Hitler's chief aide, is a popular hero along with Hitler and would qualify from the Nazi standpoint as a successor to Hitler. If not Goering, there are other determined Hitler aides who are willing and probably able to step into his shoes.

Undoubtedly a defeated and depressed Germany needed some such tonic as the Hitler program. Germans have their heads up today. There is pride in their bearing and hope in their eyes. One is glad to see that.

WORSE TRAGEDY AHEAD

But there is tragedy in the punishment that has been accorded to those who will not take the medicine. There is probably worse tragedy ahead.

I happened to be present in Hanover when there was a gathering of Hitler youth and in Stuttgart on a similar occasion. Truckload after truckload of children poured into the city for the celebration, singing and shouting.

In Hanover I stood by the side of a loyal young Nazi as a parade of a contingent of the Nazi children went by. Even he was troubled by what he heard them sing.

"Why is it," he asked, "that little girls will sing such bloody songs?"

Much of the Nazi ideology goes back to the pre-Christian era. It is being impressed on the plastic minds of children and young men. Undoubtedly Hitler does not want war now; perhaps he wants it to come never. But how, even if he wants to, can he prevent the seeds of war that are today being planted in young minds from sprouting in war 15 or 20 years hence?

Will not these same children who today ride in truckloads to feasts of Hitler youth some day become truckloads of cannon fodder bound for some western or eastern front?

Will they die vainly, as millions died vainly in 1914–1918, for a Fatherland they have been taught to love not wisely but too well?

(From The Memphis Press-Scimitar, August 10, 1933.)

As sunset gilded the medieval towers of old Rothenburg, a troop of young men, in dusty work clothers, swung down its cobblestone street.

They sang, in a strong and musical chorus, their love of their "home land."

They were volunteers of the "arbeits-dienst"—"work service"—who had been at work at road-building. Their compensation is bed and board and 30 pfennigs a day—the equivalent of a dime in American money.

In many countries young men would work for their board and keep and a dime a day. But in what other country than Germany would they march back to camp singing of their love of their "home land?"

It is a picture I will never forget, and I will think of it especially when I am disposed to criticize or condemn Germany for supporting Kaiserism and militarism and now Hitlerism.

For I think it is a key to the German puzzle.

HOME-LOVING PEOPLE

The Germans are a most home-loving people. In the course of investigating housing conditions I saw hundreds of homes of German working people. Every one of them was clean and neat. Every one of them had its little garden of vegetables and fruit trees and flowers. Every one of them had a place nearby for children to play.

The Germans are at heart a most mild and peaceful people. The vast majority don't want to fight. They want to work, to love, to raise children, make a garden, play games and swim in the sunshine, and drink beer and wine and listen to music in the evening.

That there is a minority which is spoiling for a fight is not to be denied. But if the vast majority of folks follow this minority into war-like policy, it is not for love of war, but for love of home.

The Germans are conscious of the fact that they are not

naturally warlike, but a good-natured, kindly, almost a simple
people. Because of this they fear that the homes they love are
menaced by attack from more cunning and aggressive peoples.

TO PROTECT GERMANY

They feel that Germans must stick together to protect
Germany, and let the world know that they are ready to do it.
Hence all the warlike gestures.

It could also be said that the French people also love home
above all else and do not want war, and it would be true.

But it happens that at this time it is France which, armed to
the teeth, points its guns at a Germany which is disarmed, and
sets up armed nations to Germany's east and south to hold her in
an inferior position in the world.

If only France and Germany could get together, realizing
that all the matters of dispute between them are of little importance to either compared with the imperative need of both to
avert a war which would devastate both. There is, after all, little
conflict of real interest between them. It is the mutual fear that
one has of another that drives them to absurd and tragic military
ventures. By nature they should be partners, not enemies.

WOULD SEE FUTILITY

If the French diplomats could go from city to city, and from
village to village, in Germany, as I have done, and see the men
and boys marching up and down, drilling at one time and place
without arms, and perfecting their skill with a rifle at a peaceful
"shooting match" at another time and place, and making their
bodies vigorous with exercise at still another time and place, the
whole nation bursting with new youth, life and vigor, those
diplomats and statesmen might see the futility of trying to keep
Germany permanently in an inferior position by force.

The Germans do not intend to accept forever the stamp of
being wholly to blame for starting the World War when they
contend—and historians of all countries back them up in the
contention—that Germany was no more to blame than other
nations. They do not intend to take second place to France,
Poland, and Czechoslovakia when they know they are as good as
any of them.

WILL FIND TRUE PLACE

France cannot hope to maintain an artificial condition.
Germany will find her true place of moral and physical equality

with other nations. The only question is how? By another war, or by statesmanship that deliberately rectifies the wrongs of today?

That is where America and Americans come in. Our opinion is a great weight in the European scales. It should be an informed opinion.

Hitlerism was not born in Berlin, or even in Munich. It was born in Paris, London, Prague, Warsaw and Washington.

Germany was a democratic, non-militaristic government for 13 years, but we did not back it up. The world pretended that it imposed a hard peace on Germany in order to secure the peace of the world. But it would not yield to Germany's honest plea that other nations show their sincerity by disarming down to Germany's level.

ATTACK FROM WITHOUT

Hitlerism cannot be attacked from within Germany. It can be attacked only from without. It can be attacked by removing its cause—injustice to Germany.

The world should keep faith with the German people by rewriting the Treaty of Versailles so that it really carries out the Fourteen Points on the basis of which the Germans surrendered.

Even if Germany had solely caused the war, it would be stupid and wrong to punish the rising generation for the sins of its fathers. But we now know that the other powers in Europe share the guilt equally with Germany.

The world cannot expect to see a sane, calm and tolerant Germany until the present deep injustice toward her has been rectified.

I saw with my own eyes how Hitler's opponents were being forced into silence and were being hypnotized by mass propaganda. No one could tell me that the Germans were a different breed; the same methods applied to any people would produce the same result. So, during World War II, I could write "Grand Strategy,"[1] appealing for "moral warfare", (something better than psychological warfare, which is de-

[1]See Appendix for complete text.

signed to conquer the enemy for your own purposes, whereas moral warfare would free both your enemy and yourself from the burden of war's falseness.)

I sent this appeal to free world statesmen, but none listened, and we had the tragedy of a won war and a lost peace.

IX

More Memphis Victories: The Tennessee
Valley Authority and Memphis' Own Power
System—Establishing a 12,500-acre Park
on the City's Doorstep

Seeing the state parks of Germany, I saw the possibility of
a state park for my own county, and launched a project which
was successful. We have the 12,500 acres of Shelby Forest.

(From an address to the National Conference on State Parks at Black Falls
State Park, Davis, West Virginia, Oct. 8, 1958.)

I have two vantage points to observe what needs to be done
and can be done in the field of conservation of nature and the
recreation that grows out of such conservation.

The first vantage point is the place where I live, Forest
Farm, where I have learned what being close to nature can
mean.

The second is my job, that of the editor of a daily newspaper, in the midst of human affairs.

At both vantage points, the opportunities for observation
and activity growing out of that observation are unlimited, and I
experience the embarrassment of riches.

My house sits in what our pioneer forebears called "a neck
of the woods." I know now what they meant: it is a space
between two wide clearings, with the woods coming up close on
each side. My north living room windows look to the North
Meadow and the North Woods in the distance beyond. My
south windows look to the South Meadow and the South Woods
beyond. My study window opens upon the East Woods. I know
that beyond the North Woods and West Woods lie the twelve
thousand acres of Shelby Forest State Park, where nature is

becoming primitive again, and beyond the park sweeps the giant Father of Waters, the Mississippi.

Here I live the life of Thoreau deluxe. On my morning walk I may startle a solitary deer on the trail, or a herd of them in the meadow. Or a flock of wild turkeys may spread their bronze wings at my approach and rise over the treetops in matchless beauty of flight. In the spring or summer I will waken to hear a magnificent chorus of the varied songsters known to the Mississippi flyway. In the deep of night there will come a moment when even the hoot of the horned owl or the cry of the whippoorwill—by which euphonious name I prefer to call even his southern cousin, the Chuck Will's Widow—is not heard, and this moment of perfect silence is a time when I reflect on the infinite unused possibilities open to Man. I reflect how many people could have what I have if they would but choose, and how all men could have something of what I have if only we would plan, and how all men would want it if only we would educate.

I said it was the life of Thoreau deluxe. TVA power comes on wires unseen because they are strung through the woods to the garage which abuts those woods. The wires go under the garage roof to the house and from the house in an underground cable from the main house to the picnic house where the walls are all screen; the picnic house turns its face to the all-natural woodland, and its back comfortably to the conveniences of civilization, including the telephone which I love because it keeps me in constant touch with the world of my fellow men with all their gifts to me and all their needs which I am privileged to help supply. Yes, the comforts include even the miracle of color television, where a flick of the dial may bring Shakespeare or Shaw or Rodgers and Hammerstein or Mary Chase with "Harvey", with its unseen rabbit more real than the things that are seen and another flick may shut out the vulgarities of certain popular entertainment.

We dislike cars in the mass, but how we love our own car, and I love mine, which faithfully carries me nineteen miles in a mere 45 minutes to the hurly-burly of the city and the thrills of a newspaper office, which I enjoy all the more because of the contrast with what I have at home.

My fifth-floor office commands a view of the skyline of downtown Memphis and the sunset over the river, and when darkness comes, even the neon at that distance is beautiful, and I reflect that it could be beautiful close-up, too, if only our architects would take it over and design it and bulldoze their clients into consulting them before they put up any of it. Our architects could make neon jewels in light if they would.

It is one of many opportunities I see from my second vantage point, the newspaper office. For my office gives me more than a dramatic outer view. It gives me an inner view into the hearts and minds and lives and purposes and possibilities of individuals and groups. For the daily newspaper is at the center of things. The press is the meeting ground of all the elements of society—agriculture; business; labor; the church, schools and colleges; the theater, radio and television; foundations; civic organizations; political organizations; and government in all its branches, local, state and federal. To the press they come to report themselves and to be reported; to criticize others and to be criticized; to seek the understanding and support in their endeavors such as we all crave. To the press people come to get something in or keep something out, and in doing so they tell much, and sometimes all. So the newspaper editor from his vantage point knows what is going on, and what might be going on. From this observation I have concluded this: Citizens working alone can accomplish much. Officials and experts working alone can accomplish much. A newspaper working alone can accomplish much. But citizens, officials, experts, and a newspaper working together can accomplish anything. . . .

The state park movement is a child of the national park movement, and as in the case of the Great Smoky project, a philanthropist was in the picture. Gustave Oberlaender was a German-American who had prospered as a textile manufacturer in Reading, Pa. He loved both his homeland and his adopted country, and he thought an exchange of culture between the two lands would benefit both. So he set up the Carl Schurz Memorial Foundation, to enable Germans to visit America and *vice versa*. In 1932 a group of American city officials was chosen to study municipal government, in which Germany had achieved much worth emulating. They wanted an editor interested in municipal government to be one of the party, and I was chosen. By this time I had moved to Memphis. I was recommended by Louis Brownlow, who had known me when he was city manager of Knoxville. I was his disciple. Among the things I learned from him were these two precepts:

"A good official will save his salary many times over. Pay officials well."

"People with building projects are always trying to put

buildings into parks, figuring the 'land won't cost anything.' Don't let them get away with it. If you do, you soon won't have any parks."

In the course of my studies, I visited the state parks of Germany. I thought: "If a poor country like Germany can afford a state forest park near every city, why can't rich America?

I returned to Memphis determined that our county should have one. It seemed difficult, but I remembered how the Great Smoky park had been created by citizens by (1) keeping the goals steadily before them, (2) taking one step at a time, having faith that the way would open to take the next ste.

The first step was to get the citizens. How start? It seemed best to start with the Memphis Garden Club, for this group of women had shown themselves to be unselfish and enlightened conservationists. I laid the proposition before them. They appointed a committee, headed by Mrs. W.T. Michie. That was Step No. 1. Step No. 2 was to ask the Chamber of Commerce and others to appoint an inclusive county-wide committee of representative citizens, the Shelby Forest Committee. The editor of the other newspaper was invited to be a member of the committee also.

At our first meeting we sat in a room on the mezzanine of Hotel Peabody, knowning that we wanted a forest, but not knowing how we could get it or even where it should be. Then came the first of two remarkable coincidences—or were they more than coincidences, were they examples of the truth that "all things work together for good?"

We sat, wondering how we could start? The door opened, and a big man stuck his head in. He looked embarrassed. "Hello, Jim!" cried the editor of the morning paper, George Morris, jumping up to pull Jim into the room and shake him by the hand.

"I was looking for the lumbermen's meeting, and I looked in here by mistake," he said. It was James O. Hazard, state forester.

"You're just the man we are looking for," said George, and we told him what we were trying to do.

"I can help you," said Jim. "The first thing you need is a survey of your county, to see what land you have that is suitable for forest. I will send our district forester to make the survey."

The survey was made. When the report was ready, I did an extravagant thing. Emerson says we should not fear to do extravagant things. For sometimes they turn out successfully, and then "the prudent, too, applaud."

I decided to make a lead story of that report, and put the map, which showed four areas, which were better suited for forest than for agriculture, at the top of Page One. Conventional news judgment would not have sanctioned this, but it was my judgment that our county needed a forest, and the public should know which of their lands were suitable for forest. A newspaper should sometimes make news as well as report it.

Then occurred coincidence No. 2—or was it more than coincidence. Was it rather another proof that "all things work together for good for those who plan, doubting not, but believing?"

The first edition had been off the press not half an hour before a man stepped into my office holding a copy in his hand.

"I am George Olcott of the National Park Service. I want to talk to you about this," he said, pointing the the lead story about the forest survey and the map.

"I am with the Recreational Demonstration Administration. I came here to see if your county had any areas suitable for a natural park. I have conferred with your officials and they said you had nothing. I was about to leave the city, convinced my mission was fruitless. Then I bought a copy of your paper and I saw this.

"A TVA plane is waiting for me at the airport, I will have to leave now. But I will fly over this area on my way out," and he pointed to the one of four areas which the forester had put first on his priority list. "If it looks good from the air, I will come back and survey it on the ground."

It did look good, he did come back and that area is now Shelby Forest State Park, an area of 12,500 acres only twelve miles north of the city limits. It is an area of bluff and bottom land on the Mississippi River, rapidly becoming primitive, an area so typical of the Mississippi country that the National Park Service at one time thought of making a national park of it. At the outset we would have been content with a forest of 2,000 acres, but the national officials and experts raised our sights. "Make no little plans. They have no magic to stir men's blood. Make big plans; aim high in hope and work."

I will not recount all the difficulties which you can imagine we had to overcome in the creation of a park so close to a great city. But they were overcome by the magic formula: (1) Keep the goal steadily before you, (2) take one step at a time, (3) ask

the cooperation of everyone whose cooperation you need and
have faith you will get it.

The Shelby Forest Citizens Committee, which sponsored
the creation of Shelby Forest State Park, has been succeeded by
the Shelby Forest Council, which actively promotes the right
use and development of the park and vigilantly protects it from
the instrusion of what is unsuitable.

We are working to give our Council a federated character,
so that it will have a maximum of influence. We have some
members who represent only themselves, but we have others
who represent organizations. We ask an organization to be
represented by a delegate and also by its president if possible.
Among the organizations so represented are the Chamber of
Commerce, the Council of Civic Clubs, the Jaycees, the Memphis Garden Club, the Boy Scouts, the Girl Scouts, the Memphis Chapter of the American Institute of Architects, the City
Beautiful Commission, American Legion, Tennessee Or-
nithological Society, West Tennessee Sportsmen's Association,
YMCA, YWCA, City Schools, County Schools and Parent-
Teacher Association.

When two years ágo we invited our legislators to have
dinner with us to hear the needs of Shelby Forest State Park we
could present to them a group of citizens who were a cross-
section of the city, broadly representative of various civic and
political elements. The legislators agreed to go with a group
representing our council to see the Governor. The Governor
gave us $50,000 out of his emergency funds to meet our urgent
needs and supported our program in the Legislature.

We have recently obtained these improvements: a tent
camping area, a new concession building with all-year toilets,
renovation of the public lodge, repair of the camp buildings, a
new ranger's cottage and a new horse barn.

We persuaded the Division of State Parks to invite a park
planner to make a Master Plan for our area. It locates future
improvements, but best of all it sets aside a large part of the area
at its heart to remain forever unimproved—except as the slow
process of nature improves it to make it ever and ever more like
it was when DeSoto first discovered the Father of Waters 418
years ago.

THE TENNESSEE VALLEY AUTHORITY

David Lilienthal said he needed one large city as a customer to make TVA a success. Memphis was not in the TVA

territory. But Memphis had a newspaper, ours, which was militantly for TVA. We put on a campaign and brought TVA to Memphis.

(Editorial from The Memphis Press-Scimitar, October 9, 1934.)

What Memphis Votes on Nov. 6

The people of Memphis on Nov. 6 will vote on the question whether to issue not more than $9,000,000 in bonds to build or acquire a system to distribute TVA power, which, the city's engineer, Roy Husselman, finds would give an average reduction of 45.56 per cent in our electric bills and at the same time produce enough revenue to pay taxes and to pay for the system in 20 years.

That is a question to which it would seem that there could be only one answer and that answer, "yes."

That question is: "Shall Memphis vote to co-operate in President Roosevelt's great program for the development and enrichment of the South?"

For the vast purpose of President Roosevelt in establishing the Tennessee Valley Authority had cheap power as only one of its many parts.

Right at the outset of this campaign let us clearly understand the reason for the existence of the Tennessee Valley Authority in our midst. Nowhere can we get a clearer expression than in the words of President Roosevelt himself in his message to Congress forecasting the introduction of the TVA bill:

The continued idleness of a great national investment in the Tennessee Valley leads me to ask the Congress for legislation necessary to enlist this project in the service of the people.

It is clear that the Muscle Shoals development is but a small part of the potential public usefulness of the entire Tennessee River. Such use, if envisioned in its entirety, transcends mere power development; it enters the wide fields of flood control, soil erosion, afforestation, elimination from agricultural use of marginal lands, and distribution and diversification of industry. In short, this power development of war days leads logically to national planning for a complete river watershed involving many states and the future lives and welfare of millions. It touches and gives life to all forms of human concerns.

I therefore suggest to the Congress legislation to create a Tennessee Valley Authority—a corporation clothed with the power of the government, but possessed of the flexibility and initiative of a private enterprise. It should be charged with the broadest duty of planning for the proper use, conservation and development of the natural resources of the Tennessee River drainage basin and its adjoining territory for the general social and economic welfare of the nation. The Authority should be clothed also with the power to carry these plans into effect. Its duty should be the rehabilitation of the Muscle Shoals development and the co-ordination of it with the wider plan.

Many hard lessons have taught us the human waste that results from lack of planning. Here and there a few wise cities and counties have looked ahead and planned. But our nation has "just grown." It is time to extend planning to a wider field, in this instance comprehending in one great project many states directly concerned with the basin of one of our great rivers.

This in a true sense is a return to the spirit and vision of the pioneer. If we are successful here we can march on, step by step, in a like development of other great natural territorial units within our borders.

Thus, because the people of the United States already had a large investment in the South, in Muscle Shoals, the South was selected for the investment of other millions by the Federal government to make that investment useful to the nation in a broad program of development.

The Tennessee Valley Authority is carrying out perfectly the program laid down for it by President Roosevelt. Although not a year and a half old, it employs nearly 10,000 people, doing all the things the President specified, and many more. Truly, it "touches and gives life to all forms of human concerns."

Now comes to Memphis, though it is not in, but only adjacent to the Tennessee Valley, the opportunity to be drawn within the circle of the beneficent activity of the great TVA.

Shall we seize this great opportunity?

The answer should be a chorus of ringing ayes.

(Editorial from The Memphis Press-Scimitar, October 13, 1934.)

Power Plentiful as Water

. . .Power can be, and should be, as cheap, as plentiful, as easily available as pure water is now.

It should be so cheap, so plentiful, so easily available that we would take it for granted, as we now do water.

It has meant a great deal toward civilization and "the more

abundant life" to establish the water supply on that basis. It will mean more to establish the power supply on that basis.

To make it so is the objective of the Tennessee Valley Authority.

The first step in the TVA program was to take over Wilson Dam on the Tennessee River at Muscle Shoals and thus make useful and profitable to the people this splendid property in which the people had so many millions invested.

The next step was to build Joe Wheeler Dam, just above Wilson Dam, and Norris Dam, far above it near Knoxville, and those dams are being built.

This greatly increases the worth and efficiency of the people's investment at Muscle Shoals.

But that is not all. The Tennessee River is capable of producing more power than that. So another storage dam is to be built in the Hiwassee River. Run-of-the-river dams will be built at Pickwick Landing, near Savannah, Tenn., and at Aurora Landing,[1] near Paris, Tenn. Both of these will be close to Memphis.

When these dams are completed there will be an immense store of cheap power available to the South.

That means a higher standard of living, a greater prosperity, a richer happiness.

Memphis has the opportunity to connect with this vast storehouse of power in the election of Nov. 6.

If a majority vote for the bond issue to build or acquire a plant to distribute TVA power, Memphis will then become famous throughout the country not only as a city with an abundant supply of the finest water, but also as the city with an abundant supply of cheap electric power.

If the majority so votes it will mean a big step forward for Memphis in every way.

(Editorial from The Memphis Press-Scimitar, October 17, 1934.)

Cut Down Memphis' 'Debt'

As the people of Memphis prepare to vote on Nov. 6 on the question of issuing not more than $9,000,000 in bonds to build

---

[1]No dam was ever built at Aurora Landing. Instead a big dam was built at Gilbertsville, near where the Tennessee River empties into the Ohio. Named Kentucky Dam, it backs the river across the states of Kentucky and Tennessee, creating Kentucky Lake, with a shoreline of 2380 miles.

or acquire a system to distribute TVA power, someone will surely try to scare us about taking on "such a great obligation."

Let us look at the plain, hard facts of the matter.

This bond issue is not proposed for something we do not have, and might conceivably do without. The power distribution system is here. It has been here for years.

Reducing the matter to its simplest terms, the people of Memphis have been renting that system and paying AT LEAST seven and one-half per cent net on the investment. How much more than seven and one-half per cent only the Almighty and the power people know. But there is no question about the seven and one-half per cent—the law allows that much. And that means that we are simply buying the system and paying for it—indeed, if we have not already bought and paid for it.

That leaves us with this question to be answered: Shall we keep right on paying this seven and one-half per cent and up—doubtless mostly up—or shall we borrow the money at four per cent or five per cent and buy or build a distribution system of our own? And one to which we can get title after we have paid for it.

We are going to pay interest either way, the only question is how much.

The Tennessee State Public Utilities Commission has valued the property of the Memphis Power & Light Co. for rate-making purposes at $18,258,600. Seven and one-half per cent of this is $1,369,395 a year—the "interest" that we now pay.

But it will be necessary to issue not more than $9,000,000 in bonds to build or acquire our own distribution system to distribute TVA power. The city of Memphis, because of its sound financial condition, recently was able to borrow money at less than four per cent interest. Four per cent of $9,000,000 is only $360,000 a year.

But suppose we would have to pay five per cent. To be conservative, let us figure it that way. Five per cent of $9,000,000 is only $450,000 a year. Here's how it compares:

Memphis P. & L "Debt"		Interest Rate	Interest Payment
Rate base	$18,258,600	7 1/2 pct.	$1,369,395
Cost of municipal system	9,000,000	5 pct.	450,000
Annual saving	$11,258,600	2 1/2 pct.	$ 919,395

These figures show that the city will only technically increase its indebtedness by issuing the municipal ownership bonds. Actually, these bonds will REDUCE its indebtedness.

Here is an opportunity to economize and put this city on a sounder basis which the people cannot afford to neglect.

We do not believe they will neglect it.

(Editorial from The Memphis Press-Scimitar, October 26, 1934.)

"The TVA Has Given Us Hope"

A business man of Knoxville was asked what the Tennessee Valley Authority had done for that city.

"It has given us hope," he said.

There is a reason for the hope that is in the Knoxville business men.

Not only because the coming of TVA has given employment throughout the valley to almost 10,000 people, many of these in Knoxville.

Not only because this employment has enabled many families to live normal lives for the first time since the Depression.

Not only because its purchases and the purchases of its employees have stimulated business in all lines.

Not only because vacant homes have been rented and real estate values are rising.

Not only because its rates for electricity are to be greatly reduced.

For a deeper reason than all this, there is hope in Knoxville. . . .

The TVA has given hope because it is a demonstration that democracy is not a failure and America is not running down hill.

Here are going forward mighty undertakings with a greater efficiency and without the regimentation, oppression and cruelty that is found in Communist Russia or Fascist Italy.

Here the free, indomitable American spirit which conquered the wilderness is blazing new trails toward security. For the TVA is directing the development and restoration of the resources of the Southland—water, forests, minerals—in the public interest and so correlated that they will be a PERMANENT basis of industrial, business and professional activity and prosperity.

Here is a demonstration that politics can be kept out of government activities by the simple principle of giving jobs on the basis of qualification, and qualification alone, and that when government activities are so constituted they have as little red tape, and as much efficiency and initiative, as the best conducted private business.

That such government activities do not injure, but stimulate and benefit private business which is useful to the community.

The TVA Program, when carried out, will make the South a section of conserved resources, diversified farming and industrial activities, increased wealth, so diffused as to make a widespread purchasing power and general well-being. Here is a boon which other sections envy us.

Knoxville business men like the TVA.

We predict that Memphis business men will like it, too, if the voters on Nov. 6 bring it here and give them a chance to get acquainted with its beneficent activities.

(Editorial from The Memphis Press-Scimitar, October 31, 1934)

Our Home Fires

Ras Lindemood of Union County, Tennessee, has had a fire burning on his hearth for so many years he cannot remember—since his family came over the mountains from Virginia generations ago.

His home being within the area to be flooded by Norris Lake, formed by the building of the great dam which will supply Memphis with cheap power, he will have to move. It isn't the moving he minds, but he wants to be sure that he doesn't move so far that he can't take the coals from that fire with him and keep them burning on a new hearth. This TVA will help him to do.

That hearth fire is a symbol of the ancient virtues of the pioneers. Devotion to them should be kept burning in our hearts.

As the first on Lindemood's hearth will be moved to another and a better home, so does the pioneer tradition have its continuance in the program of the TVA—daring, enterprise, co-operation, mutual help, love of liberty, hope of better things for the common man and determination to get them.

Literally, too, the TVA gives new hope for home fires. Although the homes of the town of Norris, built by TVA, have electric heaters, they also have old-fashioned wood-burning fireplaces—hearths, as every home should have.

TVA is also working to provide a bountiful supply of wood for those cheerful home fires. It is restoring our forests. It is lending its help toward the establishment of Shelby Forest right at Memphis' door.

TVA is helping to keep our home fires burning—materially and spiritually.

[Editors Note: On November 6, 1934, TVA power was voted in, and a downtown alley was named November 6 Street to commemorate the event.]

Senator McKellar was of great help in launching TVA. But he wanted to subject it to his patronage system. David Lilienthal, *The Press-Scimitar* and *The News-Sentinel* licked him. The TVA is admired by visitors from all over the world as a government enterprise. It has that admiration because its workers are chosen and governed neither by an uninspired bureaucratic civil service nor a patronage system, but by an enlightened personnel system. We had a big part in bringing that about.

X

Inner Struggles: Discovery of the Moral Re-Armament Movement—Pilgrimage to Caux: "The United Nations of the Individual Person"—Back to Church

When I came to Memphis in 1931, the *Commercial Appeal* was in receivership, having been gutted by publisher Col. Luke Lea, and our paper was in red ink, because of the destructive competition between the papers. The *Commercial Appeal* had launched an evening edition in order to fight us. Before Colonel Lea got the paper, James Hammond, an attractive, persuasive, plunging but honest promoter, saw an opportunity here to help himself by helping us. We had tried to negotiate with the receivers of the *Commercial Appeal* to get rid of the destructive competition—that is, the *Evening Appeal*—but without success. I was in that negotiation and proved I was no negotiator. But the persuasive Hammond was able to buy the *Commercial Appeal* for himself with our money, he having agreed to kill the *Evening Appeal*, the destructive weapon, if he got it. That he did, and proved to be a successful publisher in the sense of public acceptance, but not in his financial management, and so he finally sold *The Commerical Appeal* to us.

By 1936, *The Press-Scimitar* was doing well enough, not making a lot of money, but at least being well above the danger line of loss. My predecessor, Tom Sharp, always took a full month's vacation—why shouldn't I? So I planned it. The seashore is the place I like best. I wanted to spend a little time in Canada, which I had only passed through once, on my way from Duluth to Montreal. So Nova Scotia was indicated—on the sea and in Canada. And I could stop in Boston and see my old friend Mary Collson. By sea to Yarmouth, a stay at Digby, where the hotel food was tasteless. But someone said, "There's an inn run by Germans on the Atlantic coast where the food is delicious," so I went on.

I found more than good food at this inn; I met a challenge to my soul.

There was an Episcopal minister there, the Rev. Moulton Thomas—"Moe"—then of Williamsport, Pennsylvania, later of Baltimore and Trinity College. He had rented a good-sized house and operated a good-sized boat. Strange that a minister could afford such luxuries. He paid me a lot of attention. I was his guest at a meal at his home. He took me fishing on his boat in the bay.

The mystery gradually cleared. He could afford the luxuries because he was the son of a well-to-do insurance man. I got the impression that he had been, innocently, something of a playboy. Until he met Sam Shoemaker. Sam Shoemaker "changed" him and he became a minister. Sam Shoemaker had been a rather ordinary Episcopal minister until he met Dr. Frank Buchman in China. Then he became an extra-ordinary one—most extraordinary. This was the working of the Oxford Group, later called Moral Re-Armament. I had heard of the Oxford Group in Knoxville, where members of a fast society set had been changed by Dr. Buchman and gone with him on a mission to South Africa. And here I was, challenged by them. Now I understood why Moe Thomas had been paying me all that attention. I was a newspaperman, and he thought if he could win me, I would help the cause by my writings. It was something new.

"The world is not the kind of place we would like to be. The thing to do is to change it." That's not new. Karl Marx said that.

Ah, but Marx said, change it by changing the economic

system, by abolishing capitalism and the political system growing out of it.

The Oxford group said:

"Change the world by changing yourself."

That was something new. For years I and most other re-
formers had been trying to change the world by changing the
conditions and institutions of industry, of the government, in
my community, state, nation and the world. And we felt frus-
trated.

"Change yourself!"

What that came to mean! I do not remember the words
that "Moe" Thomas used, but I do know how I came to sum it
in my own words, based on what I heard from the testimonies
of many people who had been "changed:"

"So you don't like the world as you find it. It seems too
big, too out of order, too confused, for you to set right. But
there is a world of which you have absolute control—that is the
world within, the world of your own being, your will, your
mind, your spirit, your emotions, your words, your acts.
Change that world within, and how far may that very change
go to change the world without.

"How can you set that world right? By accepting absolute
standards for your life—absolute honesty, absolute purity,
absolute unselfishness, absolute love!

"Have a quiet time every day in which you don't ask God
for anything, don't tell him what to do, but listen to him, in
which you let the Divine Mind speak to you and tell you what
to do. St. Francis de Sales said: 'Listen to the Inner Voice at
least 30 minutes a day unless you are very busy—then take an
hour.' Ironic, but I think I understand what he meant. If you
are very busy, you are affecting a lot of other people's lives,
so you had better be in touch with the Mind that is Truth and
Love so you will affect them rightly.

"When you have set your own being in order, then you
can challenge others, change them, they can change others,

we have 'changed' men, changed nations, a changed world."
I was changed.

(Editorial column from The Memphis Press-Scimitar, August 8, 1955.)

CAUX, Switzerland—This is the United Nations of the
individual person. Here come men and women from all over the
world and find brotherhood with each other.

Here you see men in cheap ready-made suits or in the
handiwork of the London tailor, women in dresses of their own
fashioning or in Paris frocks. You see Hindus in turbans, Afri-
cans either in European dress or in their own native costume, a
dignified robe like a Roman toga, often made of their exquisitely
patterned and dyed cloth of their own weaving.

It is the world-wide center of Moral Re-Armament, the
movement founded by Frank Buchman, a Pennsylvania minister, first called the Oxford group. But they tell you it is not really
a movement, or an organization—it is a way of living.

The pilgrims come here seeking an answer, and most of
them go away saying they have found it. They may be seeking an
answer to the world's problems, and they find an answer to their
personal problems, too. Or they come seeking an answer to
their personal problems, and they find they can't get it except by
being part of the answer to the problems of the world.

For they don't separate the world and the individual here.
They say: stop blaming world conditions or social conditions or
the other fellow for what is wrong or unsatisfactory in your life.
Change yourself. When men are changed, the world will be
changed. Don't blame your wife, or your boss, or, if you are the
boss, the labor leader with whom you have to deal. If you are a
politician, don't blame the other party. If you are a diplomat,
you don't blame the other country—just set your own country's
policies right.

When you change into what is right, the other fellow will
note the change with surprise and gratitude, and often he will
change, too.

Four Bases of Change

And how do you change? They make it very simple. First
you decide that your life henceforth will be governed by four
absolute moral standards: (1) absolute honesty (with yourself,
with God, and your neighbor), (2) absolute purity, (3) absolute
unselfishness, (4) absolute love.

You set aside a period each day—at least 15 minutes, but usually it is much more—for a quiet time. In that quiet time, you do not tell God what you want or what He should do. Instead you listen, and let God tell you what you should do. He may tell you of some fault to correct, some wrong to make right, some good that you might do, some person you should go to see, some service you should perform. You may write these instructions down in a little book.

Then you check your guidance in two ways. Does it measure up to the four standards? If it does not, then, they say, you may be sure it does not come from God, but from your own desires. You check it with other dedicated persons; they seek guidance in advising you.

Mountain House at Caux is a handsome, huge luxury hotel. The best of food is served. There is a small paid staff, but most of the work is done by volunteers, and the service is superb. Your chambermaid may be a cultivated lady; your porter a gentleman educated at Oxford. But there is no liquor, unless some unchanged newcomer had it hidden in his grip, where I could not see it. And I have not seen a single cigarette.

There are two meetings a day, one in the late morning, one in the late afternoon, each lasting about an hour and a half. Conducted by Dr. Paul Campbell, trained as a physician, they are something like a Chautauqua, something like a revival, but mostly like nothing you ever saw before in your life.

People who are known to be ready to do so are called on to testify. A member of the German parliament may tell how, as the result of a quiet time in which he applied the four standards, he stopped playing politics with the German prejudice against the French, and sought, instead, reconciliation with the French. A South African will confess that he played into the hands of Moscow by his extreme nationalism. An American will tell how his domestic happiness was restored when he stopped blaming his wife and instead corrected himself. An ex-Communist will tell how he gave up hating and committed himself to the true revolution of changing the world thru love.

Melody and Merriment

Sandwiched in between will be jolly satirical songs, accompanied on instruments by a hillbilly-western trio from Los Angeles, the young Colwell brothers, who give their services without pay, as do so many here. Merrily and melodiously, they

will sing such songs as "If You Don't Love Your Neighbor, You
Don't Love God," sprinkled with much humor and an occa-
sional noisy slap of the wood of their instruments.

Indeed there is a lot of humor and fun in the proceedings.
People laugh at themselves and at each other. The audience
laughs frequently and gaily.

But there come the solemn moments when a person on the
platform pledges himself to give his life—all of it—to God and
his fellowman, and the audience rises to their feet as one man in
tribute and sympathy. It is a Commitment the person who made
it can't very well go back on.

It is not a new religion. There are Protestants here. There
are Catholics. There are Moslems. There are Buddhists. They
don't give up their religion. They become better Christians,
better Moslems, better Buddhists. Not a single word of theology is spoken here. Just putting into daily practice the principles
which all religions agree are good. And a warm fellowship
crossing national and creedal lines, in doing it. It adds up, they
say, to the real revolution which will save the world from
Communism—"changed men, changed nations, a changed
world."

I was not changed fully, but changed. Changed enough
that I said to myself:

"You ought to go back to church. But they say you should
be 'absolutely honest.' If you are absolutely honest, where can
you go but to the Unitarian church, for it is the only church that
doesn't have something in its teachings or its form of organization to which you cannot subscribe."

So when I got back to Memphis I joined the Unitarian
Church. When I joined I simply signed the book, agreeing to
this simple pledge:

"In the love of truth and the spirit of Jesus we unite for the
worship of God and the service of man."

What more should a Christian be asked to pledge? It is
enough for me. It is too much for some who also call themselves
Unitarians, for they are "humanists."

In that deistic Unitarian faith, believing in no superstition
or myths, I remain. But I have had spiritual experiences and

obtained a faith in God and an esteem for the mission of Jesus which makes it necessary for me to consort with the orthodox to find a faith equal to my own. I find that the orthodox, using conceptions and thoughts I cannot accept, arrive at the same unity with the same God that I have found through my liberal theology.

XI

The Latter Years and the Return to Nature

In the wilderness Jesus was tempted to seek worldly power to accomplish his good purposes. I never sought worldly power; it was given to me unsolicited and unwanted and unexpectedly. (Though perhaps the only reason I didn't want it was that I subconsciously thought I didn't have the ability to wield it, which when I got it I found I had.) But once I had it, I esteemed it over much. Though I think I always used it for fundamentally good purposes, I did allow egotism and vanity to tarnish my use of it at times, and I did over-value this shortcut to accomplishment, so that when I lost it at retirement and was compelled to rely solely on spiritual power plus personal ability and personality, I felt inadequate.

(Letter to the staff of The Memphis Press-Scimitar)

September 17, 1962

Staff:

I am no longer your boss. I am only your friend now. (I use the belitting word "only" despite the warnings we got repeatedly from our sage associate editor, the late Ralph Millett—never to use it—never say "only two people were killed." I should rather choose to be your friend than your boss, though I have tried to be both.)

Don't ever forget that I am not your boss. And don't let *me* forget it!

I will take any information or suggestions I may have regarding news or editorial policy directly to *the* editor.

But I will give some information, tips, and suggestions directly to the person who should have it, according to its nature. I will do this just as the business manager, or the circulation manager, or a bookkeeper, or a printer, or an office boy passes on something to the reporter covering the building beat, or any reporter, or the city editor, or the Mid-South editor, or the television columnist or what have you.

When I do this, you may politely give the matter no attention at all, or such attention as you think it is worth. After I give it to you, it is your responsibility to decide what, if anything, you do with it, not mine. You may or may not wish to consult your superior or someone else about it. But if any of your bosses, or *the* boss, doesn't like the use you have made of my suggestion, don't say: "It was Meeman's idea." That will be no excuse. You should not do anything about it unless it has become your idea.

I'm a pretty persistent and curious fellow, I wouldn't have gone as far as I have if I had not been, so don't be surprised if I sometimes ask: "What were you able to do with" such and such a suggestion I had made. Don't hesitate to be as frank as I have always been and say: "Nothing."

I hope we understand each other now.

Your friend,

Edward J. Meeman

cc: CHS [Editor's Note: Charles H. Schneider, the new editor.]

I was surprised to find that without the resources of a staff under my direction, and without the prestige of the position of editor, I could accomplish as much as I have accomplished.

(Editorial column from The Memphis Press-Scimitar, October 27, 1952.)

... Why does Nature reserve her grandest shows for the end of the day and the end of the year?

Nature is trying to tell us that there is no end. The sun knows he will rise again tomorrow, so he shouts with joyous colors at the finish of the day. The tree knows that she will come out green in the spring, only a little more grown, so she brings out all her banners at the finale of one year.

The sun is most beautiful at the end of the day. The tree is most beautiful at the end of the year.

Man is a part of Nature. Surely it is Nature's plan for Man that, like the day and the tree, he should know himself to be undying, and in his latter years be gay and joyous, and his life have a greater beauty and meaning to those about him.

Afterword

Much of what Edward J. Meeman believed in and worked for was accomplished before he died. The Great Smoky Mountains National Park, the Tennessee Valley Authority, Meeman-Shelby Forest State Park, the end of machine rule and adoption of a sound citizens' government in Memphis are all living memorials to his idealism, energy and acumen.

Yet much remained to be done. In one of the last letters he wrote before a stroke crippled him the last few months of his life, Meeman demonstrated his remarkable ability to discard and adapt, synthesize and digest—in short, to edit—the ideas with which his life brought him into meaningful contact. The letter, written in June, 1965 to a friend, in Tryon, N.C., in answer to questions about Moral Re-Armament, is a succinct statement of his own "formula" for saving the world. If he had lived longer, he would certainly have altered it again, but out of the thought and experience of 76 years he was able, like the great editor he was, to find "what is most significant," to add "what is necessary for completeness," and to arrange "the words in the order that they can best be understood and valued."

The letter read in part:
.. . I met Peter Howard on several occasions, and he spoke to a joint labor and management discussion group of which I was chairman. Yes, a big, able man. MRA is good, but too narrow. It

is not an all-embracing ideology which can save the world. We need all these in one package:

1. MRA with its four absolutes and daily quiet time for guidance.

2. Christian Science with its emancipating ideas that God is all, wholly good, everywhere present and available under all circumstances, that Man is the expression of this God, and the healing and solution of problems that follow this conception.

3. The Quaker idea of unselfish service.

4. Ecumenicity—recognition that all religions are inspired, each relatively true, and having a common ground of universal truth.

5. Proliferation of small, intimate prayer groups, as organized by Faith at Work, Inc., and Laymen's Movement for a Christian World, for intimate discussion of practical religion and intensive prayers, sometimes around the clock, that heal diseases often declared incurable.

6. Capitalism, now suffering not from decay as many believe, but from arrested development, brought to maturity by the universal practice of profit-sharing. (This would have prevented the rise of Communism, and this is the dynamic, accompanied by the other points herein, which can destroy Communism.)

7. Federal Union of the free self-governing, democratic nations which guarantee personal freedom, within the larger United Nations.

8. Invigoration of democracy by unselfish citizens' organizations devoted to establishing good non-political local government.

9. Unselfish participation as members also, by nearly everybody, in political parites.

10. Back to Nature and the simple life—and saving Nature so it will be there to come back to.

That's my program for saving the world.

I feel optimistic this evening, just having returned from presiding as president of the Memphis Committee on Community Relations (race) at an off-the-record conference in which a leading department store put in writing what they always intended to do, give equal employment, and the NAACP agreed to withdraw their pickets.

What a work of art in flowers and grasses that of Lucy's!—I am very grateful.

All good to you both.

Sincerely,
Ed

That letter was the final distillation of the Trinity of Relationships which had concerned and motivated Meeman all his life—the relationships between man and man, between man and his natural environment, and between man and God. Earlier, in concluding an address to the University of Florida at Gainesville on January 14, 1949, he had offered to the world a more complete summation of those ideas and ideals in what he called "the first draft" of a "Freedom Manifesto." Along with his Grand Strategy series during World War II, he considered it one of the major works of his career. (The complete texts of both the Grand Strategy articles and the Freedom Manifesto may be found in the Appendix to this volume.)

In accordance with his wishes, Edward J. Meeman's remains were cremated and his ashes buried at Forest Farm in order that he might, in Walt Whitman's words, "return to the eternal uses of the earth." A short distance away from the farm and from Meeman-Shelby Forest State Park, the 12,500-acre conservation and recreational facility which he almost singlehandedly got set aside for his fellow citizens, there now stands the materialization of the last of his dreams for them. It is the Garden of the Ever Living, which he conceived as "the only perfectly decent, sensible, thrifty, poetic, religious and sacred—in a word, the only perfectly civilized—method of disposing of the human body that the world has ever seen."

It is a tract of trees, grass, shrubs and flowers, laced with foot trails, set aside under the terms of his will for the burial of the ashes, cremated elsewhere, of those who, like him, wish their bodies to "return to the eternal uses of the earth."

There will be no monuments, no headstones, no labels on any burial spots, only the eternal trees and grass and flowers and, at the edge of the garden, a place where funerals or memorial services may be held.

The Garden of the Ever Living was founded after his death by the Edward J. Meeman Foundation, which was established by Meeman and chartered by the State of Tennessee in 1949 as "a scientific, educational and charitable trust for "the conservation of natural resources, the preservation and promotion of the principles of democracy, and the promotion and furtherance of good journalism."

The first Meeman Foundation trustees, in 1949, were Edmund Orgill, former mayor of Memphis, Lucius E. Burch, Jr. and Hunter Lane, Jr., attorneys; the late Gilmer Richardson; and Meeman himself.

In 1976, the trustees were: Orgill, president; Burch, vice president; Clinton R. Pearson, public accountant, secretary; Lane; and J. Z. (Zollie) Howard, retired managing editor and associate editor of *The Memphis Press-Scimitar*.

The Meeman Foundation inherited, after individual bequests to many employes, the major part of Meeman's estate of somewhat over $2-million. Major grants by the Foundation trustees between 1967 and 1976 were:

$36,000—University of Tennessee, to endow annual awards, established by Meeman, for best editorials and best public service by Tennessee newspapers, presented in conjunction with the Tennessee Press Association; also to finance annual critiques of contest entries by Tennessee newspapers in several categories, including editorials and public service.

$59,000—Boys Clubs of Memphis, for promotion of conservation and of democracy.

$738,777—Southwestern (College) at Memphis, to aid in construction and operation of a Center for Continuing Education.

$200,000—University of Tennessee, to endow pay for visiting journalistic lecturers and supplement the pay of distinguished journalism professors at the U-T College of Communications, and to endow two international journalism fellowships annually at the Communications College, the fellows, when possible, to be selected from NATO countries.

$250,000—Memphis State Universtiy, to aid in construction of building for its Edward J. Meeman School of Journalism.

$300,000—Memphis State University, in the form of

Meeman's 612-acre Forest Farm, conservatively valued at this figure, to be used as a retreat for college conferences and as a perpetual wilderness area for biological study and conservation practice.

$250,000—LeMoyne-Owen College of Memphis, established more than 100 years ago as an institution to serve Negroes, as a contribution to its building fund.

$100,000—Tennessee Conservation League, for its conservation work in the state.

$205,000—Southern Newspaper Publishers Association Foundation, to endow Edward J. Meeman Annual Workshops for discussion by Southern journalists of professional problems.

$175,000—Scripps-Howard Foundation, to endow annual conservation awards to American newspaper people for conservation writing and cartooning, in national contests. Awards totaled $5,000 a year when established by Meeman. Grant enables doubling of annual awards, to $10,000.

But the poor immigrant's son who started his newspaper career at $4 a week and left more than $2-million to his fellow men left them an even greater spiritual legacy. The thing he knew with the greatest certainty was that Man must find ways to live in harmony with Nature or perish forever from the Earth. In one of his most profound and prophetic writings, here reprinted from the September 1961 Rotarian Magazine, he expressed both the challenge and his own confidence that it would be met:

THE EARTH—MAN'S ETERNAL HOME

I swear there is no greatness or power that does not emulate those of the earth!

I swear there can be no theory of any account, unless it corroborate the theory of the earth!

No politics, art, religion, behavior, or what not, is of account, unless it compare with the amplitude of the earth.

Unless it face the exactness, vitality, impartiality, rectitude of the earth.
          —Whitman

It took Nature billions of years to prepare the earth as a home for man. When the work was completed, it was seen to be good. The Earth contained every opportunity and every challenge that Man should desire. The safe land and the perilous sea; rugged mountains and fertile plains; and everywhere that climax of Nature's scene, the age-old forest, ever renewing and enriching itself.

In a few thousand years, Man has laid waste the earth. America, a scene of especial variety and richness, Man has needed but a few centuries to despoil.

It was said formerly that Man was but a puny thing against the great relentless power of Nature. Today Man is not puny in his power over Nature. In the country, he has laid low the forests and left gaunt gullies in their places, and the good soil washes to the sea; in the cities, hard brick and concrete cover the gentle earth, between the cities, vast junk heaps are piled up from the misuse which Man has made of the wealth and beauty which were his legacy from Nature.

No, Man is not puny in power. He is puny only in wisdom.

His growth in power has outrun his growth in wisdom. He has befouled his own nest. A befouled nest drops to earth and by the beneficent processes of Nature, soon becomes clean, soft earth again. But foul sores and the giant scars made by Man on the face of the Earth can never be entirely healed. Man is destroying his eternal home.

"Let's have a road here." The shoulder of a mountain is dynamited. Concrete (which "grows harder and whiter with age") is laid down. That mountain can never be the same again. It is forever scarred, and must remain so through all the millions or billions of years that Man will dwell here. Was the road needed? Perhaps. But what if it were not needed? Then what a crime! The Earth is not yours, O Man, for your own moment of time. It belongs to all men of all the aeons. Be careful what you do to it, for what you do to it is irreparable!

"Let's straighten this stream." The giant steam shovel is brought in. The winding stream, flowing clear over rocks between trees and grass, becomes a foul, muddy canal with caving banks. The fish which gleamed in its clear waters are no more.

"Let's build a factory here; the river will make a convenient sewer." The dark black waste is poured in and the stench rises.

"Let's cut down this forest; it will make shacks for our slaves in the cities." And having cut down part, we toss away a careless cigarette and the rest of it is gone. Gone beyond repair, because with the trees has gone the humus, which is to the earth as precious and as destructible and irreplaceable as the fine-textured cheek of a beautiful woman.

"Here is a spring; what a good flow!"—and we encase its sweet lips with concrete and pipe.

"Let's drain this swamp; it will make a nice farm to raise some more food for our fat bellies." The sun beats down and what was cool, rich ooze, breeding and sustaining manifold life, bakes and cracks into desolate chips. Where are the reeds and the lilies? Where shall abide the turtle, the goose, the crane, the swan?

Let man turn within and find eternal life, and the conscience and grace which say: "I live not today for myself and my own times alone; I love and act and refrain for all men and all time. I will save the beautiful Earth for the uncounted men and the uncounted years that come after me."

Then we shall begin to conserve and restore. We shall recognize that this primeval forest is the veritable Garden of Eden, which we abandoned in our folly, and to which we return. For it was with primeval forest that God covered the earth before He said: "It is finished and it is good." It was the final boon that He gave to His children; but we destroyed it as a child breaks his toys. We shall set aside the primeval forest where yet it remains, but we must not be content with that. We must restore. We must carefully plant all the varied growths that made up this primeval forest and patiently wait until Nature restores something near to the likeness of what we did not appreciate. It will take centuries; but we must know the amplitude of time.

We must never set explosive or drill to earth without knowing: "This is forever," and asking, "Have we the right?"

Awakened and enlightened Man shall turn to his junk heaps, those excreta of civilization, and by his chemistry convert them into the materials for articles of human use, or else into good clean earth again.

He will cleanse his streams and see them sparkling in the sunshine, again fit for Man and fish to disport in. Even the self-cleansing ocean will not be a dump—he will love it too much so to insult it. The Beach, where life began and today returns in the final flower of cosmic consciousness to contemplate the beauty of the universe, will gleam white in the sunshine of a redeemed Earth. This same sunshine, touching the trunks of the trees rising behind, turns to gold the columns of what was Man's first and will be his last temple—the Eternal Forest.

To these words today all mankind is pronouncing a fervent Amen.

—Edwin Howard

Memphis, Tennessee
1976

Appendix I
Grand Strategy

(From The Memphis Press-Scimitar and other Scripps-Howard newspapers, December, 1942.)

The recent successful invasion of North Africa was important, not only because it gave us a real basis for our hope of victory, and reason for believing that it would come earlier than anyone had a right to believe before this success was achieved, but because it was a demonstration of the effective employment of the only strategy by which victory when it is won, can be made real and lasting.

Statesmanship, when it employs war, does so as a last resort, and wages it with but one objective: to make friends of enemy nations. Until you have made a friend of your enemy, you have not won the war, for while the enemy is still an enemy you remain at war with him, and your victory is not conclusive. If it were possible to "destroy" the enemy nation, that would not be victory, because the victor nation could not live with himself and with history after such an act.

The first phase when the Statesman employs Power in the form of military force, is to win the support of friendly neutrals by demonstrating that his nation deserves to win and has the strength to win. The second phase is to win unfriendly neutrals. The third phase is to detach satellite allies from the main enemy or enemies. The fourth and final phase is the employment of overwhelming force, undeniable good faith and positive assurances, to detach the people from the government of the main enemy or enemies.

Opening of Third Phase

The North African campaign was the brilliant opening of the third phase of the war. By infinite patience and the infinite pains which is genius, by the magnificent mobilization and use of great force, the Allies, led by America's Franklin D. Roosevelt, were able to win the French in North Africa over from a neutrality which was in effect collaboration with Hitler to active participation in the war on our side. This is true Statesmanship, which has given the democratic world the truest reason to be proud of ourselves and our leaders that we have had in a long time.

Shall we be great enough to employ the same statesmanship to "defeat" and win over, in order, Italy, Germany and eventually and finally (though with the greatest difficulty), Japan?

This is the greatest question before us—greater even than any questions of production or of purely military strategy.

For if it is our policy to deal with the Italy controlled and misrepresented by Mussolini and the Germany controlled and misrepresented by Hitler with the same insight, faith, patience and long view that were demonstrated in dealing with a France controlled and misrepresented by Laval, that is not at this time apparent to the public.

We Repudiated War

After World War I the Western Liberal democratic peoples came to a profound disbelief in war. They believed that it was not only barbarous, cruel, un-Christian and destructive of civilization, but that it was the most uncertain weapon a nation could employ. It was easy to embark on war, but once embarked on, war became uncontrollable. War released forces that could not be calculated in advance; it took directions that were unplanned by those who waged it. "Never again!" was the determination of these democratic peoples.

But there arose in Italy and Germany leaders who voiced a contrary belief in goodness, glory and efficaciousness of war. They had before them the example of Japan which had never sincerely disavowed war and had made steady gains by it. Yet Japan had paid the Western democratic nations the compliment of moving slowly, stopping after each assault to see if the Western nations would translate their disbelief in war into action to stop its use by Japan.

First, Fascist Italy, then Nazi Germany, made war. Mussolini in Ethiopia, Hitler in Czechoslovakia, found the pacific democratic West unprepared to resist their aggression. The Western world continued to hope that this anachronism of tyranny and brutality in Twentieth Century Europe would blow up.

But Norway, the Low Countries, and France were invaded and conquered. Then the Western world recognized that it must mobilize all its resources to meet force with force on a tremendous scale. That we are doing.

Our Judgment Upheld

As we are engrossed in waging war, it is not surprising that we should have failed to observe, or at least to appreciate, that in this very war our former judgment on the uncertainty of war as an instrument of policy has been proved to be correct. Mussolini, by making war, has lost his empire and doomed his regime to decay or overthrow; whatever the outcome of the way, he will have no prestige with either winner. We have not yet won the war, but Hitler has already lost it. The central doctrine of his philosophy is the pre-eminence of the white race. By loosing war, Hitler has enabled Japan to drive the white race out of much of the Far East; to suffer a loss of prestige which it will be difficult to regain even with victory. He aimed to give Germany primacy in Europe; by attacking, enslaving and torturing Germany's neighbors he has made it difficult in the future for Germany to exercise the leadership in economic and cultural affairs which Europe would have been willing, perhaps eager, to accept from a civilized Reich.

What to Believe

If we of the liberal democratic West are to avoid a similar irony, we must recognize now that it is not for us to adopt a belief in war, but to cure the people of dictator lands of belief in it, insofar as they still do believe in it. It would be tragedy if, by waging war, we came to a belief in the primacy of war as an instrument, a failure to see that we have a more efficacious instrument at our command whenever we choose to use it.

An enlightened man knows that not to support the war is treason to his country. But he also knows that not to recognize the tragic limitations of war, and the uncertainty of achieving its goals even in victory, is treason to himself, to his country, to civilization and to God.

Moral Victory First

In the first winter of World War II, when there was little fighting and we called it the "phony war", there was speculation whether there had not been a return to "classic" strategy, in which the rival forces were ranged opposite to each other with engagements of only small forces, and the result was determined by seeing which side could mobilize the greater strength, without their coming into total conflict with all the mutual destruction that would involve. The invasion of Denmark, Norway and the West proved this conception was not true.

Yet that conception has tremendous possibilities for us now.

The war we are now waging in another sense will be a "phony war" if it is based on the false idea that military victory precedes rather than follows moral victory.

Not Just Incidental

True, we have used moral statements, but up to date they have been but the little brother of force—a minor ally. Not that we have been hypocritical; we have not; we have been sincere. Just as sincere as the Army and Navy are when they treat the chaplain with respect. But the chaplain is but a mere incident in the real business at hand. The chaplain is a moderating influence, a comforter. But he is not the ruling spirit. Our Atlantic Charter and the speeches of our statesmen, fine though they have been, have little above the status we give to our chaplain. At long last, our production problems are being solved and we are passing the ammunition. But we are not yet trusting in the Lord.

Until Spirit and Mind become supreme; until Love becomes our commander-in-chief; until physical force falls into place as the mere instrument of these Kings of Life, we shall not win. We cannot conquer the Nazis if we share their faith in the prior power of force. For if we share this faith, they shall have become our conquerors, though they lie prostrate and broken on the battlefields.

Nothing has yet been said by any of our statesmen to equal Lincoln's

"*With malice toward none, with charity for all.*"

It will not serve to have something said as great as this. Something must be said that is greater. Let us have words which will lift the human spirit out of the hell it has made to win victory over itself—"everywhere in the world."

Two Extremes to Avoid

It is a mistake to think we can slacken the war effort while we spin dreams of a post-war world. It is an equal mistake to think we can "win the war first" and then build the kind of world we want. What we can do and must do is to unify war aims and war-making with war-making subordinate and responsive at all times to the aims of war. Since war, though necessary now, is demonstrably the most uncertain of means, we should subordinate it to what is certain—moral change.

The world cannot rescue itself from Naziism unless it rescues Germany from Naziism.

Our supreme objective to which all military objectives should be subordinated is to bring about a return of legitimate, responsible, humane and civilized government in Germany—a government with which we could make peace. For peace is the only objective which a civilized nation can have in making war.

Toward this objective we should wage mighty moral warfare.

Not "Psychological" War

We do not mean "psychological" warfare. We do not refer to propaganda which might spread panic among the people of Germany, resulting in universal civil war and chaos. Such propaganda is only a mental form of physical force. Use of it would make it only more difficult to bring into action the superior moral force through which alone we can find victory over the world's disease. Use of "psychological" warfare would only intensify the unwholesome conditions which gave birth to the Nazis, and we should only have exchanged one evil for another. We mean a propaganda for which propaganda is not a suitable name. We mean an appeal which will bring the Germans not to confusion but to their senses—an appeal to that element in Germany which never deliberately chose Hitler as their leader and government; that element which is still aware of that great civilized past of cultured, Christian, philosophical Europe— aware of it because it was schooled by it and at heart is yet a part of it.

Unless we recover that past, we can have only a blasted future. For mankind must find its unity in time as well as space; the ages as well as the lands of earth must be knit together.

Is it possible, while war is being waged against the Nazis, to appeal to that element in Germany which never indorsed Hitler and his gang, and through that element, bring the German people as a whole to their senses?

Let us see. In forming an opinion on that question, it will be enlightening to consider our own recent history. Since 1940 our American nation has undergone a revolution in its state of mind: from a belief that we could obtain security through peace and a resolve to remain at peace, to a belief that we must make war and that we must acquire a warlike spirit.

We looked at conditions in the world and said: "They won't let us function thru channels of peace; we must make war." And then we revolutionized our outlook and our economy. If it is true—and it is—that Germans have substantially the same physical, mental and spiritual makeup as ourselves, they are capable of a similar revolution of outlook. Our statesmanship can bring them to the conviction: "The world won't let us function thru channels of war; we must have peace," and this conviction would impel them to revolutionize their outlook and their direction. This is the kind of revolution we should wish to bring about in Germany, for it is the only kind of revolution that will profit us . . . a revolution that brings civilization, order and that free trade in goods without which there can be no free trade of ideas, not a revolution which will bring to Germany and Western Europe a chaos and bolshevism worse than any we have seen.

Hitler Thrust on Them

We must recall what we are so inclined to forget: that a majority of the German people never chose Hitler. He was given the chancellorship by President Hindenburg; he used the chancellorship to set up a dictatorship and fasten himself on the people by methods of force and fear. In the last free election in Germany Hitler got only a third of the total vote. That vote was cast after years of bitter depression which had made people desperate. More significant is the fact that in 1928, when Germany was enjoying a brief prosperity, Hitler's vote had shrunk to a mere 3 per cent. Under normal conditions the German people rejected Hitler.

Many if not most of those who voted for Hitler did not believe he would be what he has proved to be. If the outside world believed, as it did, that Hitler was not really formidable, and that anyhow responsiblity would sober him, it is reasonable to believe that is what many Germans who voted for him thought. Even that third which voted for him did not foresee what he would to to them and to the rest of the world. Many of them, desperate in poverty, thought Hitler was a useful bogey-man whom they could employ to frighten the world into giving them a more important place and greater economic opportunity. They did not know that the bogey-man was a genuine devil who would bewitch their nation into shame and disaster.

Other Considerations

If after Hitler had seized power, the German people seemed united behind him, let us not forget what fear of a concentration camp will do. If at least many of them seemed enthusiastic, let us not forget what a price human nature in any land is willing to pay for economic betterment—and, we are told, Hitler had "ended unemployment," "gave Germany order, self-respect," spruced her up. Before we cast into outer darkness the Germans who fell for this line, let us remember how very many Americans in the twenties admired Mussolini extravagantly because he "made the trains run on time." To bring it closer home, let us not forget that the people of a great American state, Louisiana, seemed for a time to be willingly accepting the domination of that cruel and ruthless American dictator, Huey Long; that he was making progress toward the seizure of adjoining states by his storm troops, that had it not been for the election of Franklin D. Roosevelt and his decisive measures which lifted this country out of depression, it might have happened here—"Der Schoene" Huey might have taken over the White House. Even today, the people of certain American cities submit to boss rule, though they have the freedoms with which to free themselves.

Beware Of Crowd Thinking

So that there may be an understanding of crowd thinking, I commend to statesmen of today a study of Gustav LeBon's "Psychology of Revolution," which is still valuable, but should be supplemented by the later and more liberal Everett Dean Martin's "Behavior of Crowds."

Whatever was the acceptance of Hitler's peacetime program, the testimony of correspondents leaves no doubt that the majority of the German people did not want war. Hitler said he would keep them out of war, and they believed him. He said that the purpose of the vast war preparations was only to back up his diplomacy, and they thought that it was true. Munich was as great a relief to the German masses as to any other European people.

Once the war was on, it is true, the cruelties and horrors ordered by the Nazi leaders were participated in and condoned by many Germans. War psychology releases the primitive and brutal in man. When to war psychology you add the feeling of racial superiority, with which the Germans were impregnated by systematic Nazi propaganda, the result is sure to be outrages committed on peoples who are falsely regarded as inferior. This is not a German but a universal phenomenon. Our own decent ancestors had the saying "the only good Indian is a dead Indian" and acted out the saying. Lynching is still a phenomenon of American life, participated in by citizens who are normally kind, decent and respectable. Crowd psychology, particularly as it is released by revolutions such as the Communist, Fascist and Nazi revolutions, is a subject worthy of the study of all statesmen and citizens. Let us not condemn those possessed by the demon of revolutionary crowd psychology, but let us break up the crowd mind where it has been formed, and prevent its formation in the future by measures of statesmanship.

Signs That Ground Is Fertile

An indication of the possibility of arousing active opposition to Hitler in Germany is the general skepticism within Germany toward Hitler's victories, apparent long before the Allies displayed any military strength or success. The lack of enthusiasm with which the German crowds greeted these military feats, which the world at the time regarded as remarkable, the general conviction of the German civilians that military success, dazzling though it was, was not enough to win the war for Germany and bring the much desired victory—these are signs that there are mature people behind Nazi lines, to whose good sense we should appeal to help us overthrow the Hitlerism monster.

By enlisting the enemies of Hitler within Germany on our side, we can bring about the downfall of Naziism more quickly, shorten the war, save American lives, and make the victory we shall win a lasting one.

How could the German people have made the tragic mistake, not of choosing Hitler, for a majority never did, but of giving him a tolerant ear, to the extent that he was able to seize power?

The German mistake lay in believing that the depression from which they were suffering was due to defeat in war. They did not see that it was due more to the effects of war itself, than to defeat. They did not see that Americans were suffering, too, from war-caused depression.

The democratic countries turned against war in the period after 1918, because being victorious, they knew that victory does not wipe out the price that must be paid for war. The German people did not make as complete a turn away from war as we did, because, being defeated, they believed their economic misfortunes were due to defeat rather than to the tragic consequences that follow all war for victor and vanquished alike. It was this discrepancy in thought—as well as the militarism that is undoubtedly a factor—which made Germany much more a prey to war than the rest of the world—though even there a majority of the people never wanted or expected actual major conflict.

Is the liberal, democratic, civilized Germany which was overwhelmed by the wave of hypnotizing Hitlerism still there behind the monstrous facade of Naziism?

Yes, it is still there, waiting for Statesmanship among the United Nations to bring it forth.

That is the testimony of the last correspondents to leave there.

Another Germany

Says Louis P. Lochner, chief correspondent of the Associated Press, in his book *What About Germany?* (Dodd, Mead & Co.)

. . . There is another Germany. It is a Germany which is submerged and inarticulate at present because every possibility of public utterance has been taken from it. It is a Germany which prays for deliverance from the Nazi yoke as fervently as any member of the United Nations can pray for the end of Hitler and his system. It is a Germany which still cherishes the normal civilized ideals of equal and humane justice for all; of honesty and truthfulness in human relations; of sympathy for the oppressed, the weak and the infirm. It is a Germany which is ashamed and humiliated at the disgrace into which Naziism has dragged the German name . . .

After citing at length examples of anti-Nazi feeling and activity, Mr. Lochner says:

*I would not be honest if I did not emphasize the fact that all
these revolutionary groups were anxious about United Nations
guarantees of good faith in their expressed sympathy for "The
Front of Decent People."*

*These groups were unanimous in testifying that their one
great obstacle in spreading anti-Nazi propaganda was the fear of
wide masses of the German people that the peace which would
follow this war would be even farther removed from the promises
of the Atlantic Charter than the Treaty of Versailles was removed from Wilson's Fourteen Points, on the basis of which they
had trustfully laid their fate in the hands of the Allied and
Associated Powers.*

*How to overcome this doubt is something over which the
best minds in our nation might well ponder. Either we admit the
existence of "another Germany" or we do not. If we deny it (this
would be an indication of stark political blindness on our part),
the war will be prolonged indefinitely, and even the most rabid
anti-Nazis will fight to bitter end, realizing that there is no hope
for the decent element in Germany anyway. If we recognize its
presence—even though we think it too weak for the moment to
count as a political factor—we should encourage it in every
possible way. To say that all Germans are alike is playing
Goebbels' game, as he has warned possible revolutionaries that
their defection will not help them as the outside world recognizes
only one Germany.*

*I say with all the conviction at my command that anything
we can do to encourage that "other Germany" whose modest
beginnings I have tried to trace, should be done. This includes a
willingness to supply the guarantees that the sponsors for the
Front of Decent People in Germany deem necessary.*

Receptive Audience

Frederick Oechsner, Central European manager of the
United Press, in his book, *This Is The Enemy*, (Little, Brown &
Co.) says:

*On the propaganda front we must contribute to undermin-
ing the enemy's morale and his will to fight. There is a large and
receptive audience to be reached in Germany on a basis of
frankness and accuracy. The United States, a comparative newcomer in the war, is in an extremely good position to take
advantage of this audience, conducting a psychological attack
step by step with the military and economic attack. For anyone*

who has lived in "propaganda conditioned" countries, the importance of this side of warfare can scarcely be exaggerated.

It would be pointless to base our war or peace aims on "annihilating" or "wiping off the map" a German nation, which, shorn of its vassals, numbers 60,000,000 members. In fact, they must not only be allowed to help in the reconstruction of a Europe which they have brought to its worst plight in centuries; they must be made to help with the energy and ability which they unquestionably possess.

Open to Suggestion

Says Howard K. Smith, in *Last Train from Berlin*, (Alfred A. Knopf):

The minds of the vast majority of the German people are open to suggestion. The evidence that they are ready for an alternative is overwhelming. Why has the Gestapo seen fit to set up arsenals in residential Berlin? Why were the Storm Troops dissolved and why does Hitler constantly strengthen his personal army, each member of which is sworn to die, not for Germany, but for him and Naziism? Or why have the Germans who listen to foreign radio broadcasts multiplied in number in six short months? The answer to all these questions is not that the German people are going to revolt tomorrow, for they have nothing to revolt for, but that they are open to suggestion! But nobody makes any suggestions. Telling them in our wireless propaganda that the Nazis are bad is as utterly stupid as the politics of those "Peace Leagues" which used to tell the world that peace is a good thing. Everybody knows that peace is a good thing, what people want to know is how to get peace. The mass of the German people have realized that the Nazis are not a good thing, but what else is there? They are open to alternatives, but nobody offers any. The only alternatives they know are: win with the Nazis and save themselves from the horrors of defeat at the hands of a world which hates them, or lose with the Nazis and suffer those horrors. A fate apart from the fate of Naziism is contained in none of our promises nor our propaganda. Instead, we offer them Mr. Kaufmann and the sterilization of the whole German people. And so the German people fight and offer their lives to save their families—and incidentally the Nazis—from total destruction; and they work their hands to the bone to make the guns the Nazis need. And the war will go on for a needless number of years because the German people are afraid.

Our attitude toward Germans is too much governed by our belief in a concept called the "German Mentality." Our idea is that there is a certain twist of mind which is born into Germans, which inevitably makes them warlike and want war. Let jingoists and brass-band-patriots hold their spleen. I am not trying to whitewash the enemy. I agree that there is this kind of mentality which is inducive to war. I agree that wherever it is discovered it should be annihilated by merciless brute force. I agree that it exists, and in the course of this book, I have been trying to point out where it exists and which minds possess it. They are: (a) the old Prussians, the militarists and the armsmakers alike. Krupp has it. Von Rundstedt, Von Bock and Von Leeb, the Blitz Triplets, have it, and with them, hundreds of thousands of other stiff-necked, bemonocled "vons." My considered recommendation is sudden death by the firing squad, or the noose, or the ax. (b) Hitler, Ley, Goebbels, Goering, Ribbentrop have it. Himmler and his hundred thousand young men who would kick their grandmother's teeth out if Himmler ordered it, have it, too. There lies the War Mentality. War is their education, their religion, and their food and drink. They are destructive, anti-social, diseased, warped and utterly useless to this world of men. They must be destroyed, and one need not be finicky about the methods.

But I deny that there is any war mentality in the mass of the German people. The German people do not like war any more than we do. Who was scared stiff during the Munich crisis? Not Hitler, Goering and Himmler; they were just itching to hear the heroic music of cannon-fire and bursting bombs. They were probably a wee bit disappointed when Chamberlain gave in so easily, but, doubtless they promised themselves to do better next time. But the German people were paralyzed with fear. More than the victimized Czechs or the British. Remember when after the World War the British slogan was Hang the Kaiser? Well, however strange it may sound, I am entirely in favor of the Hang the Kaiser policy. It was a good one. But why in the name of common sense, did we not carry it out and hang the Kaiser and all he stood for? Why didn't we hang the Prussian generals, and Krupp, Thyssen, Von Borsig, Huebermann and perhaps half a million or so others? Anyhow, we didn't. We left the hard-fisted old men to thrive, to have their spirits mellowed one day by the creamy words of a brown-shirted paranoiac, and free to start another war. Instead of hanging the Kaiser, we hanged the German people. We were like the doctor who opened up the side of a patient for an appendectomy, but became confused and cut out the patient's stomach instead of his infected appendix. Let's discover our error before the operation, instead of after it, this time.

I know that it is unpopular to say so at this moment of tension and hate, but it is true that there is still lots of good solid stuff in the German people. If we intend to win not only the war, but also the peace, and set up a new and better world, a lot of Germans are going to be among its best components. A lot of Germans are just aching to help make a better world. In order to win them from Naziism to our side and end the war sooner, we've got to offer them a part in the better world. Thus far, we have not done so. Whatever the virtues of our leaders, Roosevelt, Churchill and Stalin, their 13-point program, which the two former created and Stalin subscribed to, is not definite enough, and does not make clear enough the inclusion of the German people, minus Naziism, in the scheme. Stalin's recent statement to the effect that the "German people must pay" has not helped the situation any, nor has Eden's subscription to that slogan. I repeat again that this is only my personal opinion: but I am convinced of its validity, and, since I am writing for readers in a democratic country, I am entitled to express it and to try and win converts. I know full well how hard it is for the Russians to conjure up an attitude of constructive forgiveness toward people who make the shells and bombs which have wrecked their land and killed their hard-working citizens; and I know how hard it is for British subjects who have suffered torture under Nazi bombing raids to stifle a well-earned desire for vengeance. And, certainly, I am not asking for a softening of our military attacks, by air, land or sea against Germany. In fact, I want to see the Germans beaten until they howl and scream with anguish. I know these things. But, also, after long, close experience with the German people, I know this: unless the British, the Russians and the Americans offer, with deep sincerity, to the German people another way out besides life or death with Naziism, this war is going to last for an unnecessarily long time, and the Germans, to avoid their horrible fate, are going to fight it with the reckless spirit of men who have absolutely nothing to lose but their lives! Every time we call for the annihilation of the German people as our only war aim, we are actually pouring gunpowder into Nazi cannon to be shot at us. I suggest giving the German people something more important than their lives to lose— namely, a better place in a new, better world—and I will wager

*anything that the European war will be over within a year after
we have adopted and carried out the scheme!*

Most of us believe that Germany, if victorious, would never
be able to retain a hegemony over the occupied countries by
force, but would succeed in dominating Europe only if she won
the little countries to voluntary allegiance. Then how can we
expect to handle Germany by force alone? The use of force is but
half the battle; winning her heart is the other part—the part we
have not yet undertaken.

It is to our interest to win the German people to our side. If
they are utterly crushed and demoralized, bolshevism will
triumph there, and the sole power in Europe will be Russia.
There still remain in Germany embers of traditional European
civilization—its culture, its religion, its private business
enterprise—which can be fanned to new life. We do not want a
balance of power in the old cynical sense, but we do want a new
world order based on powers which are in balance. It will be
very uncomfortable for Britain and us in the new association of
nations if Russia is the only great power on the continent of
Europe.

Right Attitude to Russia

Mr. Roosevelt and Mr. Churchill are statesmanlike in the
creative faith by which, it seems, they hope to change Russia
from the aggressor nation she showed herself to be in her
wanton and ruthless attack upon Finland, and her bargain with
Hitler, and to make her instead a pillar of the peace system. I
believe this policy, which is similar to the one I advocate in our
relations with Germany, can be successful. But even a Russia
which has been cured of aggressive desires should not be allowed to dominate the affairs of western Europe, as will be the
case if Germany should be destroyed or bolshevized. If Germany should be destroyed or bolshevized, there would be
created that imbalance which causes future wars. Our interests,
our duty to civilization, impel us by diplomacy to bring into
being in Germany a government which is both anti-Hitler and
non-Communist, for that is the only kind of government with
which we can make a secure peace and have dependable relations.

War Within a Great Family

This is a civil war, a fratricidal war between western nations
which should be co-operating with each other. Perhaps it is

more accurate to call it a matricidal war that Hitler has pro-
voked. For Germany is the central land of Europe, of which all
other lands partake. The Anglo-Saxons, the dominant strain that
has made England, the primitive fathers of democracy, were
Germans who came from the heart of Germany. The German
people are a fusion of all the races around them—Scandinavians,
Slavs, Alpines, Franks (French), Dutch. If the people of Germany are damned by the nature of their blood, then all Europe
is damned, for the German blood is a composite of all the bloods
of Europe. But, fortunately, science tells us that it is not so. The
Germans are a great people which our arms and our statesmanship must free from the low estate into which Hitler has brought
them. As Paul Hagen says, Germany was the first of the countries of Europe to be "occupied by Hitler." We must consider it
simply as the last of the countries which it is our job to set free
from his brutal tyranny.

A Precedent Exists

The same faith and patience which President Roosevelt
showed toward France should be shown toward Germany. It
may have the same fortunate results in hastening American
military victory and saving American lives. Whether it works or
not, it is still the only right and prudent thing to do. If it is
necessary to win France, it is even more necessary to win
Germany, for Germany is the greater prize.

Effects of Extremism Here

I was born and schooled in the North, where I was given
the idea that the Civil War was a crusade by the North against a
South which had committed the sin of slavery and the crime of
secession. I came South, where I have lived for more than 20
years. I have learned that if the South sinned against the Negro,
the slave-trading North was a party to it. I have learned that
Abolitionist extremists in the North enabled the extremists in
the South to prevent the moderates in the South from freeing
the Negroes, as I believe they would have done if the North had
kept its moral fervor at home, where there were enough evils to
correct that it need not have remained unemployed. Moral
indignation—what crimes have been committed in thy name! I
have learned that the South has not yet recovered from the
Reconstruction—that peace of vengeance which the North imposed. I have learned that the whole nation has suffered terribly
from that ignoble and stupid peace. Not until the Franklin D.

Roosevelt administration—honor to it for that!—did the nation begin to remove the colonial status it has imposed on the South. I do not want the world, including ourselves, to suffer from similarly ignoble and stupid treatment of Germany.

If we do not intend to impose a stupid and vindictive peace on the German people, let us say so now, in such clear and unequivocal terms that decent Germans will come to the aid of the cause of the United Nations.

Wanted: A Great Spirit

Let us try to find a Robert E. Lee in Germany—in all likelihood there is one. Let's find a Lincoln on our side—in all likelihood there is one. Will Franklin D. Roosevelt be that Lincoln? Let largeness of spirit meet largeness of spirit and heal a world sick to death.

Impossible? The impossible has just been done. After the fall of France it was "impossible" that Britain could hold out against Nazi might. But Britain did that impossible.

Today we need a spiritual battle of Britain. Tiny Britain had a serene confidence that she could not be conquered. We need to have a similar confidence that the seemingly helpless spiritual forces of religion and civilization can by their own intrinsic might overcome the forces of revolution, paganism and barbarism which now have Germany in their grip—but are not themselves Germany.

World's Only Hope

The hope of the world—the only hope—is that we can avoid a third world war by ranging a preponderant armed force on the side of justice and order. We conceive that such a force could remain unused because its presence would prevent outbreak by an aggressor, (as Japan would have drawn back in 1931 had the United States and Britain joined forces to prevent her aggressions.) The best hope of establishing such an enforced peace is to establish it NOW—by ranging overwhelming force to bring about the downfall of the criminal regime and the establishment of a legitimate government which can restore justice and order within Germany, a government whose word we can trust and with whom we can make an honorable and secure peace.

Force Won't Suffice

Force will bring about the downfall of Hitlerism in any event. But only convincing promises of a peace without vindictiveness can bring about the establishment of a sane and honorable government in Germany. For only a type of German who would be looked upon by decent Germans as a kind of quisling would accept and co-operate in an unfair peace, which punished the innocent with the guilty. The realities of patriotism are the same in every country, and we must have imagination to see that any German who is honorable enough to be worthy of our trust will not surrender if surrender means the dismemberment and crucifixion of this country.

> *"Breathes there the man with soul so dead*
> *"Who never to himself hath said,*
> *"This is my own, ny native land!"*

A dead soul which does not feel the patriotic sentiment has no honor, either.

As to Italy and Japan

If this policy is adopted toward Germany it will obviously also be adopted toward Italy. The problem of Japan, although more difficult than that of Germany, can nevertheless be solved in similar lines, once peace with Germany has released our forces for a showdown in the Orient. There is a liberal and Christian element in Japan also, which we should encourage and to which we should appeal, though it is, of course, not as strong or deeply-rooted as in Italy and Germany, for Christian civilization there has not had as much time to establish itself.

Power Plus Love

Americans are willing to sacrifice the flower of American youth, the seed of our future national strength, if that is necessary to our survival. But if through having more than military strategy we can minimize that sacrifice patriotism demands that we adopt that "more."

Statesmanship is the union of Power and Love. Love without Power is futile. Power without Love is horrible, and a horrible failure. Power and Love when in balanced unison, succeed.

By using moral warfare as our supreme weapon, of which military strategy is the supporting weapon, and only thus, can be obtain Victory which is truly that.

Appendix II
The Freedom Manifesto

For the last 100 years, the world has been dominated by the Communist Manifesto, issued by Marx and Engels in 1848. True liberalism has been under attack from Marxism from without. As the democratic nations have been weakened by human fifth columns, so the democratic philosophy has been weakened from within by the poison of Marxist conceptions, and related statist conceptions.

By its fruits, shall we know this philosophy. The Marxist century has ended with half of the world in slavery and the other half in fear.

We are, in this year of 1949, starting a new century. Let us make it a century of hope.

Let us, in this year of 1949, issue a Freedom Manifesto. The Communist Manifesto led mankind to slavery and despair. The Freedom Manifesto will guide the world to liberty and hope.

Let me propose a basis for the Freedom Manifesto.

Proposed Basis of The Freedom Manifesto

We proclaim the Free Society.

Let us begin with the economic, since economics is basic. We do not accept the Marxian theory that Man is animated only by materialistic motives. We do not believe that ideas and ideals are only an expression of a pre-determined economic system; but we do believe that ideas and ideals which do not find expression in the way we work, buy, sell, distribute and consume are vain. So we express freedom in our economic life.

Marxism teaches that one economic system succeeds another in automatic evolution—slavery, feudalism, capitalism. Marxists claim that capitalism is destined to be followed by socialism or collectivism which is to be the final and permanent system. This we deny.

Economic Diversity

There is no need to accept, or reason to choose, a society dominated by one economic form. In our Free Society, various economic forms exist side by side, in competition with each other, and flourish as they meet human needs and conceptions of the good life; they diminish as they do not meet these needs.

In our free society there is self-employment—the person who employs himself repairing radios, or watches, or automobiles, or making by hand furniture, or baskets, or hats, or cookery. Perhaps we should have more self-employment: certainly it should be recognized as one of our permanent and valued economic forms, and the doors should be always wide-open to it for those who like it and can make it pay.

There is the partnership.

There is the co-operative, where a group of people join forces to produce, to see, or to buy.

There is the corporation. Corrections are needed in corporate structure and practice. Stockholders should have more voice and take more responsibility. Workers should share profits and have a sense of owning and helping. Perhaps, even, corporations need to develop and perhaps can develop, souls. However, which of us would want to live in a society without corporations? Not everyone wants to work for himself, or in a cooperative, or for the government, or to depend on such forms to meet all his needs. There are things which the corporation can do better than any other economic form. So the corporation is permanently one of the economic forms in our free society.

There is government or public ownership. Public ownership is sometimes inefficient, sometimes bureaucratic; but there are economic activities which government—municipal, state, or national—can do better than a co-operative or a corporation. So we will have government ownership in our free society. We shall get away from bureaucracy and inefficiency by an extension of the TVA idea. That is, through the government corporation instead of the bureau, through regionalism instead of centralization in the capital, we shall induce government enterprise rather than mere government operation. In such government enterprise, employees are under a personnel system, oppressed neither by political uncertainty nor by the dead hand of unimaginative civil service; they may find careers, promotion and security such as they would find with a well-managed private corporation.

However, government operation is only one of our economic forms; it is not a social corrective of ills that may exist in other forms. Law, not collectivism, is that corrective.

No Final Decision

In our Free Society, we never make a final decision as to how much of one economic form we shall have and how much of another. If a government operation is not working well, the people will not hesitate to sell it to a corporation or a cooperative. If it is indicated that a corporate activity should be under public ownership, the people will not hesitate to buy it. Experience and sense of values, not dogmatic theory, will determine their decisions, and decisions are always subject to review. We find what is better by never-ending thought and experiment. However, changes from one form to another are made without confiscation, and without harm or loss to individuals.

Private Property

The right of private property is fundamental.

The institution of private property is not evil; it is a positive good. Property is necessary to the freedom and dignity of man. A propertyless man can have spiritual freedom and dignity, but not complete freedom of movement, activity and enjoyment; he cannot be an effective citizen in a vigorous democracy. If property is not owned by individuals, it will be owned by the state, and the state will thereby become a dictatorship. We need to have property more fairly acquired, more widely distributed, and more securely held against loss and confiscation. High taxes from war and excessive governmental activities are one form of confiscation. A free society requires that most of its citizens shall be responsible property owners.

Labor Movement

With such a conception of the need of private property, the labor movement will necessarily change its strategy. Instead of moving on and on in the industrial field toward the confiscation of profits, it will see them as a necessary thing. It will strive to increase the property holdings of the workers it represents. Under a system in which private property is becoming ever more widely held, the workers represented by labor unions would become owners of stocks in their own and other industries. Workers should become owners; owners should be workers. Thus we can attain a stability under which society will not move, with "the inevitability of gradualness," into a centralized socialist state.

Reserves

Under such a system there should be few periods of recession or depression.

However, corporations should build up reserves for pensions and for employment, in order to avoid lay-offs or discharges in slack times. This will minimize dependence on government and strengthen the property system.

But no security outside oneself can equal the security of ownership of property in a system in which property is made secure.

The ownership of property by individuals, and the building up of private savings reserves should be that reliance.

Decentralization

A healthy rural life is the foundation of a free society. A family living on its own acres is the ideal.

We favor the decentralization of property, of industries, of population. Our cities are too big. They should be remade to make possible more wholesome living. Bring the country to the city, as we have already brought urban comforts to the countryside. Eliminate smoke, smells, noise and traffic hazards. Bring to the country the interest and variety of the city; to the city dweller that self-expression that comes from working with growing and living things.

Mass Production

Mass production should have brought Man freedom from drudgery, not slavery to mechanism and to artificial appetites for unneeded things or cheap satisfactions. The object of mass production should not be something not needed or to be thrown away after a brief use.

The commercial manufacture of food and clothing outside the home, the commercial performance of services for the individual which the individual should do for himself has been carried too far. We need to do more things for ourselves with our own hands.

Exaggerated, high-pressure advertising is illegitimate. Man is not a consumer. He is not a waste container for industries whose wheels dare not stop. Industry is a servant whose wheels turn at the command of Man to satisfy his needs. We are not slaves of the industrial machine.

Political Democracy

Freedom depends on a vigorous political democracy also. Citizens should take responsiblity for government in their counties, towns, and cities. When citizens' committees, without selfish motives, organize permanently to maintain non-political council-manager government, as is done in Cincinnati, they are accepting their responsibility. Then there is no room for a boss.

Union of the Free

We do not despair of the United Nations. We wish to continue our efforts to make it ever more and more effective as the organization of our "one world." But we put freedom first. Freedom is fundamental. If freedom is to be preserved and extended in the world as a whole, then the nations which have long practiced freedom must federate. They must have a common policy in international affairs, a common defense force, a common currency, common citizenship, and a customs union. Therefore, we favor a Federal Union, not merely a military alliance, of the Marshall Plan countries—those contributing and those receiving. Those are the United States, Canada, Australia, New Zealand, Union of South Africa, Eire, Great Britain, and the democracies of Western Europe. We favor a great Union of the Free, and we urge that the first steps be taken now. If the present crisis which threatens freedom should pass, it will still be necessary, in order to avert or to cope with future dangers, that the free nations be permanently united with each other. To the great Union should be added other states, from time to time, as they wish to join and can qualify through having established within themselves the practice of freedom and democracy.

Man

In order to bring into being and preserve this Free Society, we must have men who are determined to remain free, and who know how to remain free. There is nothing wrong with the nature of Man. He need only awaken to what he really is, and live in the fullness and perfection of his true nature. He was made for dominion over a self and a world which offer him satisfaction and joy. Man is the expression of God, the fulfillment of the Divine Being. When man lives at one with God, and wields God's infinite power, he will not desire any puny power over other men. He will not submit to any human being so foolish as to wish to lord it over him. Here is the key to human freedom.

How shall we get such men, such citizens for our Free Society? By cultivating them. The principles are laid down in all religions. Religions do not agree on the reasons why men should be good, but they substantially agree on what men should do. The need is to get these teachings practiced. This can best be done by forming groups or circles of laymen in each faith to meet with each other to study the practice of religion and to encourage each other in that practice. It is useful also to form "cells" which cut across denominational lines for the encouragement of the practice of individual responsibility for freedom.

Thus men will be trained to live and help other men to live in the sunlight of freedom in the joy of that self-expression which belongs to all the sons and daughters of God.

For the correction, completion, enrichment, and activation of the Freedom Manifesto I invite the communication and co-operation of all men and women everywhere who love freedom.

INDEX

ews Service

HOME

THE WEATHER
Fair and slightly colder today; Monday
increasing cloudiness with rising tem-
perature.

PRICE FIVE CENTS

Vol. XLIII—N

The Editorial We
A Posthumous Autobiography
by Edward J. Meeman
Compiled, Edited and with an
Introduction and Afterword by
Edwin Howard

Edward J. Meeman for 31 years made the
The Memphis Press-Scimitar one of the
most influential newspapers in middle
America. For 25 years before that, he was
a reporter and managing editor on the
Evansville (Indiana) *Press,* reporter for the
Terre Haute (Indiana) *Times* and the
Newspaper Enterprise Association, and
founder and editor of the *Knoxville* (Tennessee) *News-Sentinel.* During those years
he developed, tested and dedicated himself to the ethical principles and public
service policies which were to make him
and *The Press-Scimitar* great forces for
local, regional, national and international
good during the 1930's, '40's, and '50's.

It was Meeman who put the National
Park in the Great Smoky Mountains, put
the authority in the Tennessee Valley Authority, and took the "Boss" out of Boss
Crump through his persistent news fea-
tures and editorials. It was his leadership
that got the Wilderness Bill and the Land
and Water Conservation Fund Bill
through Congress in 1964, a fact recognized by the National Wildlife Federation's bestowing its Communications
Award on him that year.

His guiding principle as a crusading
editor is expressed by a maxim he
formed, tried and repeatedly proved:
"Citizens working alone can do much;
a newspaper working alone can do
much; citizens and their newspapers
working together can do anything."

Mr. Howard has brought together from
more than fifty years' files and published
material ample evidence to support the
validity of the maxim.

In The Pictures

These scenes, taken by
Sam's Creek last Friday afternoon, are typical of mile
after mile of logging operations of the Little River Lumber company in the Middle
Prong of the Little River
tract of land which lies in the
heart of the Smoky Mountain
national park area, and is
owned by the people of Tennessee.

1. When the timberin
crews and their skidders finish with a mountainside ar-
moved up to a fresh stand of
virgin timber, nothing is left
but a tangle of brush and
logs, with here and there
on a ridge, a few trees strip-
ped of their branches and in
most cases with the tops
knocked off.

2. By the state's contrac
with the lumber company,
10-inch trees and everything
of lesser size were to be left
standing, but as this scene
shows, not even shrubs, eve-
green, laurel or moss was
saved.

3. At the head of the pre-
ent operations up Sam
Creek, the picture shows
a skidder in the midst of its
destruction.

4. A skidder puls by
company is compelled
gather up the debris an
burn it to prevent
forest fire which woul
destroy the 15-inch tim-
ber and over which is be
standing. But the timberin
methods of the Little Rive
company have their adva
tage. Forest fires are n
feared because no damage
could be done, no trees exce
devil ones having been lei
standing.

5. Ten-inch trees were
have been spared.

6. Col. Townsend told
News-Sentinel reporter la
week that small trees do n
exist among large ones. ani
for that reason no 15-inc
trees could be found after th
large trees had been logge
The trees in the backgroun
just beyond the first op-era-
tions, seem to indicate ot
erwise.

RICH MIDDLE
RUINED BY T

By JOHN T. MOLTOUX
More than half of the Middle Prong of the Little River
Lumber Co. tract, owned by
the state of Tennessee, in the
exact center of the national
park area, is already in ruins.

The pictures taken two days
ago, give only a faint idea of
the destruction that has come
in Lynn Camp prong for a
distance of six miles beyond
Tremont, Sam's Creek for a
distance of a mile and a half
beyond Tremont, and which
awaits Thunderhead, the third
of the three main creeks
which unite at Tremont to
form the Middle Prong.

The despoliation of Lynn
Camp prong has been going
on for about two years and
has about reached its end.

Sam's Creek was still virgin when this reporter and a